BUILDING BRIDGES

BUSINESS COMMUNICATION FUNDAMENTALS

DR. R. REXMART

To God Almighty, Jesus Christ, for guiding me with divine strength and wisdom; to my father, Mr. C. Ravikumar, whose support has been my anchor; to my mother, Mrs. N. Mercy Mabalet, for her endless love and encouragement; and to my sister, Ms. R. Rayona Mace, for believing in me every step of the way. This book is a reflection of your trust and inspiration, which have made my achievements possible.

Contents

Contents

Contents

Foreword

It is both an honor and a privilege to introduce **Building Bridges: Business Communication Fundamentals**, authored by my esteemed colleague, Dr. R. Rexmart. As an Assistant Professor of English at the Faculty of Science and Humanities, SRM Institute of Science and Technology, Dr. R. Rexmart has consistently demonstrated a commitment to advancing the understanding of effective communication in today's context.

In today's rapidly evolving global marketplace, the ability to communicate clearly and effectively is an essential skill that transcends job titles, industries, and cultures. Dr. R. Rexmart's book serves as a vital resource for students, professionals, and anyone interested in sharpening their communication skills to navigate the complexities of the business world.

Drawing on a wealth of academic knowledge and practical insights, Dr. R. Rexmart meticulously explores the fundamental concepts of business communication. The chapters are structured to guide readers through the intricacies of both verbal and written communication, offering useful strategies that promote clarity, persuasion, and relationship-building. His approach is both analytical and practical, encouraging readers to apply theoretical insights to real-world scenarios.

What sets this book apart is Dr. R. Rexmart's emphasis on the importance of empathy and understanding in communication. He recognizes that successful business interactions require more than just the exchange of information— they depend on the connections we forge with others. By fostering critical thinking, he equips readers with the tools needed to bridge communication gaps and foster collaboration in diverse environments.

"Building Bridges" is not merely a textbook; it is an interactive guide that encourages self-reflection and skill development. As a fellow educator, I believe that this book will inspire readers to become not only better communicators but also more effective collaborators and leaders.

I wholeheartedly recommend this work to anyone seeking to enhance their business communication skills. It is a compelling read that promises to be a valuable addition to your personal and professional library.

Congratulations to Dr. R. Rexmart on this significant contribution to the field of business communication. I am confident that this book will enlighten and empower many on their journey toward effective communication.

Best Wishes!
Dr. R. Blessy
Assistant Professor of English
Faculty of Science and Humanities
SRM Institute of Science and Technology
Ramapuram, Chennai.

Preface

In an increasingly interconnected world, the ability to communicate effectively in business is more crucial than ever. **Building Bridges: Business Communication Fundamentals** is designed to equip readers with the essential skills necessary for navigating the complex landscape of modern business interactions.

Whether you're just starting your career, seeking to enhance your skills, or aiming for leadership positions, this book serves as a comprehensive guide to mastering the art of communication in a professional setting. From understanding the nuances of verbal and non-verbal communication to mastering the art of persuasive writing, each chapter is crafted to provide practical insights and actionable strategies.

Effective communication resonates value and it can be applied immediately in the real-world envirionment. In a time when businesses thrive on collaboration and innovation, the ability to exchange ideas clearly and confidently is a bridge to success.

As you embark on this journey through the fundamentals of business communication, we hope you discover new perspectives, refine your skills, and uncover the importance of building bridges—connecting not just words, but people, ideas, and opportunities.

Welcome to your path of becoming a more effective communicator and building lasting relationships in your professional endeavors.

Acknowledgements

I am profoundly grateful to God Almighty, whose guidance and inspiration have been the foundation of my journey as an author and educator. This book, **Building Bridges: Business Communication Fundamentals**, is a testament to the knowledge and insights I have gained throughout my academic and professional life.

I extend my heartfelt thanks to my academic mentors and teachers from **The American College (Autonomous) in Madurai** and **The Scott Christian College (Autonomous) in Nagercoil**. Your dedication to shaping young minds and fostering a love for learning has profoundly influenced my path. I would like to give special recognition to **Dr. A. Linda Primlyn** ma'am, whose encouragement and wisdom have left an indelible mark on my educational journey and inspired me to pursue excellence in communication.

To my former colleagues at **Malankara Catholic College, Mariagiri**, and **Sri Krishna College of Arts and Science, Coimbatore**, thank you for the collaborative spirit, camaraderie, and unwavering support we shared. The experiences and discussions we had enriched my perspective and fueled my passion for teaching.

I am equally appreciative of my current colleagues at **SRM Institute of Science and Technology, Ramapuram**. Your collaboration and enthusiasm have made it a privilege to be part of such a vibrant academic community, where the pursuit of knowledge and effective communication thrives.

To everyone who has contributed to my professional development, your influence has been invaluable, and this book is as much yours as it is mine. Thank you for believing in the importance of bridging communication gaps and for being a part of this journey.

Prologue

In the realm of business, success is not solely determined by the products we offer or the services we provide; it is often shaped by the conversations we have and the connections we forge. Communication is the lifeblood that courses through the veins of any organization, linking departments, inspiring teams, and fostering innovation. Yet, despite its paramount importance, effective communication remains one of the most challenging skills to master.

Building Bridges: Business Communication Fundamentals aims to unravel the complexities of communication in the business world, transforming it from a daunting task into a strategic advantage. As we delve into these pages, we will explore the fundamental aspects of communication, highlighting how clarity, empathy, and adaptability can enhance not only individual performance but also the collective success of an organization.

Throughout my years in the business sector, I have witnessed firsthand the remarkable difference that effective communication can make. I have seen teams flourish under leaders who could articulate their vision and drive motivation with their words. Conversely, I have also observed talented individuals struggle due to misunderstandings, misinterpretations, and a lack of coherent dialogue. It is this dichotomy that compels me to share insights and techniques that can empower you to become a more confident and impactful communicator.

As you embark on this journey through **Building Bridges**, remember that every conversation is an opportunity—an opportunity to connect, to inspire, and to drive change. With each chapter, you will gain tools to break down barriers, foster collaboration, and create an inclusive atmosphere where ideas thrive.

Let us begin building bridges together, forging connections that will ultimately lead to a more dynamic, innovative, and successful future in business. Your journey toward becoming a master communicator starts here.

Editor Note

Building Bridges: Business Communication Fundamentals, authored by Dr. R. Rexmart, is a vital contribution to business education, especially in today's interconnected world. This book explores essential communication skills necessary for success in diverse environments, emphasizing clarity and relevance. Dr. Rexmart's insights create a rich tapestry of concepts and practical strategies, empowering readers to master effective communication. As you engage with this work, you will discover the importance of crafting resonant messages, navigating cross-cultural interactions, and fostering collaboration. May Building Bridges guide you in developing the foundational skills needed for successful business relationships, bridging gaps, and thriving in your professional journey.

Dr. Rakesh Babu M
Assistant Professor
Department of English
Malankara Catholic College, Mariagiri
Kaliyakkavilai, Tamil Nadu.

ONE

INTRODUCTION TO BUSINESS ENVIRONMENT AND COMMUNICATION

In the rapidly evolving world of business, understanding the environment in which a company operates is crucial. The business environment refers to the combination of internal and external factors that influence a company's operations, decision-making, and overall success. Effective communication is integral to navigating and thriving within this environment. Let's explore both concepts in detail.

The Business Environment

Definition:

The business environment encompasses all external and internal factors affecting a company's performance. It includes economic, social, technological, legal, and competitive dynamics.

Types of Business Environment:

- **Micro Environment**: Refers to the immediate surroundings that directly affect a business, such as customers, suppliers, competitors, employees, and stakeholders.
- **Macro Environment**: Encompasses broader societal factors like economic trends, political conditions, technological advancements, social changes, and ecological issues that indirectly impact the organization.

Factors Influencing the Business Environment:

- **Economic Factors**: Interest rates, inflation, employment levels, and economic growth directly influence business operations and consumer behaviour.
- **Social and Cultural Factors**: Demographics, lifestyle changes, education, and cultural trends dictate consumer preferences and workforce dynamics.
- **Political and Legal Factors**: Regulations, trade policies, and political stability are crucial for compliance and strategic planning.
- **Technological Factors**: Innovation and technological advancements can disrupt markets and create opportunities for businesses to grow and adapt.

Importance of Understanding the Business Environment

- **Strategic Planning**: Awareness of environmental factors enables businesses to formulate effective strategies to exploit opportunities and mitigate risks.

- **Adaptability**: Understanding changes in the environment helps organizations adjust their strategies to remain competitive and relevant.
- **Decision-Making**: Informed decisions can be made by analyzing environmental influences, leading to better resource allocation and planning.
- **Risk Management**: Recognizing potential threats in the business environment allows companies to develop contingency plans and safeguard their interests.

Communication in Business

Definition:

Business communication is the process of sharing information and ideas within and outside the organization. It includes verbal, non-verbal, written, and digital forms of communication.

Types of Communication:

- **Internal Communication**: Involves the sharing of information among employees and departments. This can include meetings, emails, reports, and team briefings.
- **External Communication**: Involves interactions with clients, suppliers, and the public. Examples include marketing materials, press releases, and customer service interactions.

Importance of Effective Communication

- **Clarity and Understanding**: Clear communication ensure that messages are accurately conveyed and understood, reducing the likelihood of misunderstandings.

- **Team Collaboration**: Good communication fosters a collaborative work environment, enhancing teamwork and collective problem-solving.
- **Customer Relations**: Effective communication with customers builds trust and loyalty, improving satisfaction and retention.
- **Crisis Management**: In times of crises, effective communication is crucial to address concerns, provide updates, and maintain transparency.
- **Brand Image**: Consistent and positive communication shapes a company's reputation and contributes to brand building.

Challenges in Business Communication

- **Cultural Differences**: Global businesses face challenges due to language barriers and varying communication styles based on culture.
- **Technology Overload**: The proliferation of communication tools can lead to information overload, making it difficult to focus on key messages.
- **Misinterpretation**: Messages can be misunderstood or misinterpreted, especially in written communication where tone and intent may be unclear.

Understanding the business environment and mastering effective communication are vital for both individual and organizational success. Companies that stay attuned to environmental factors and prioritize clear and constructive communication are better positioned to adapt to changes, engage stakeholders, and achieve their objectives. As business landscapes continue to evolve, these elements will remain integral to sustainable growth and competitiveness.

TWO

MODELS OF COMMUNICATION

Models of communication help to explain how messages are transmitted and understood between individuals or groups. Here are some key models:

1. **Shannon-Weaver Model**: Developed in 1948, this model is one of the earliest and most influential. It consists of the following components:

- Sender: The originator of the message.
- Message: The information being communicated.
- Encoder: The process of converting the message into signals.
- Channel: The medium through which the message travels (e.g., spoken word, email).
- Decoder: The process of interpreting the received signals.
- Receiver: The individual or group receiving the message.
- Noise: Any external interference that can distort or hinder the message.

2. **Berlo's SMCR Model**: David Berlo's model (1960) emphasizes four components:

- Source: The communicator who has the information.
- Message: The content, structure, and elements of the communication.
- Channel: The media used (sight, sound, touch, etc.).
- Receiver: The target audience who interprets the message.

This model underscores the importance of each element in effective communication.

3. **Schramm's Model**: Wilbur Schramm proposed a model focusing on the shared experiences and fields of experience of the communicators. It involves:

- Encoder: Transforms thoughts into messages.
- Interpreter: The capacity to make sense of the communication based on shared contexts.
- Decoder: Converts the message back into thoughts.

Schramm emphasized the role of feedback and the shared background between parties.

4. **Interactive Model**: This model, unlike linear models, recognizes communication as a two-way process. Elements include:

- Sender and receiver roles interchange.
- Feedback is crucial to understanding.
- Context and noise significantly affect communication.

This model reflects real-life conversations more accurately.

5. **Transactional Model**: This model posits that communication is a simultaneous process where senders and receivers collaborate. Key features include:

- Continuous feedback.
- No clear distinction between sender and receiver.
- The role of context and environment shapes the interaction.

Transactions of meaning happen in real time, making it dynamic.

6. **Barnlund's Transactional Model**: Dean Barnlund expanded on transactional models by highlighting continuous movement:

- Communication involves multiple senders and receivers.
- Each interaction consists of verbal and non-verbal components.
- Understanding evolves as messages are continually processed.

7. **Westley and MacLean's Model**: This model emphasizes media and mass communication and is complex:

- It reveals how varied messages reach multiple audiences.
- It highlights the interactions between various media channels and the audiences they serve.

8. **Helical Model**: Proposed by Frank Dance, this model visualizes communication as a spiral process:

- Communication builds over time, expanding in complexity.
- Past experiences shape current interactions.
- As individuals communicate, their understanding and skills evolve.

Each model offers unique insights into the complexities of communication. Understanding these can greatly enhance our interpersonal skills, media literacy, and overall effectiveness in sharing information. By tailoring our approaches based on the framework that best fits our situation, we can improve clarity and connection in our communications.

THREE
7Cs of Communication

The 7Cs of Communication are a set of principles designed to improve clarity and effectiveness in communication. They serve as a framework for creating clear, concise, and impactful messages. Here's a breakdown of each of the 7Cs:

1. **Clarity**

- Definition: Ensure that your message is clear and easily understood.
- How to Achieve: Use simple language, avoid jargon, and be specific about the main idea. Clearly outline the purpose of your communication.

2. **Conciseness**

- Definition: Keep your message as brief as possible without losing meaning.
- How to Achieve: Eliminate unnecessary words, repeat information, and irrelevant details. Use short sentences and stay focused on the core message.

3. **Concrete**

- Definition: Provide solid facts, details, and examples to support your message.
- How to Achieve: Use specific data, relevant anecdotes, and clear examples. This approach helps make your message more believable and impactful.

4. **Correctness**

- Definition: Ensure that your communication is free of errors in grammar, spelling, punctuation, and factual information.
- How to Achieve: Proofread your messages, verify facts, and use appropriate language for your audience. Correctness builds credibility.

5. **Coherence**

- Definition: Your message should be logical, organized, and flow well.
- How to Achieve: Structure your communication logically, with a clear beginning, middle, and end. Use transitions to connect ideas and maintain a clear line of reasoning.

6. **Completeness**

- Definition: Include all necessary information for the receiver to understand and respond effectively.
- How to Achieve: Anticipate the needs of your audience and address any potential questions. Provide all relevant details, context, and background as needed.

7. **Courteousness**

- Definition: Communicate in a friendly, respectful, and considerate manner.
- How to Achieve: Use polite language, show appreciation, and be empathetic to your audience. A courteous tone fosters positive relationships and encourages open communication.

Application of the 7Cs

In practice, applying the 7Cs can significantly enhance communication in various settings—whether in personal interactions, business correspondence, or public speaking. Here are a few tips for applying the 7Cs effectively:

- Planning: Before communicating, outline your message using the 7Cs as a checklist to ensure that all elements are covered.
- Feedback: Seek feedback from peers or listeners to gauge clarity and effectiveness.
- Revisions: Don't hesitate to revise your message based on the 7Cs to enhance accuracy and impact.

The 7Cs of Communication serve as an effective guide for improving communication skills across different contexts. By integrating clarity, conciseness, concreteness, correctness, coherence, completeness, and courteousness into your communications, you can enhance understanding, foster engagement, and build relationships. Whether you're writing emails, giving presentations, or having conversations, applying the 7Cs can lead to more effective and positive interactions.

FOUR

FORMAL AND INFORMAL COMMUNICATION

Formal and informal communication are two distinct ways that information is conveyed within organizations and social interactions. Each has its own purpose, structure, and context. Here's an overview of both forms:

Formal Communication

1. **Definition**: Formal communication refers to the structured and official channels of communication used within organizations. It typically adheres to predefined protocols and is often documented.

2. **Characteristics**:

- Structured: Follows an established hierarchy or framework (e.g., organizational charts).
- Official: Associated with business, legal, and governmental contexts.

- Written or Verbal: Can be in written forms such as reports, memos, and emails, or verbal forms like meetings and presentations.
- Clear and Concise: Aims for clarity and precision, reducing ambiguity.
- Record Keeping: Often documented for legal and historical purposes.

3. **Types**:

- Downward Communication: Information flowing from higher levels of management to lower levels (e.g., directives, policies).
- Upward Communication: Feedback and information sent from lower levels to higher management (e.g., reports, suggestions).
- Horizontal Communication: Information exchanged between peers or departments at the same level (e.g., interdepartmental meetings).

4. **Examples**:

- Company-wide emails announcing policy changes.
- Formal reports submitted to management.
- Scheduled meetings with agendas.

Informal Communication

1. **Definition**: Informal communication refers to the casual, unofficial way information is shared. This type of communication often develops naturally within a workplace or social group.

2. **Characteristics**:

- Personal: Based on relationships and social interactions rather than formal structure.
- Spontaneous: Occurs on the fly, without pre-planning or structure.
- Flexible: Lacks rigid protocols; can be adapted to the context.
- May Be Unrecorded: Often consists of verbal exchanges or non-documentary forms.

3. **Types**:

- Grapevine Communication: Rumours and informal news circulated among employees.
- Social Interactions: Casual chats, lunch break conversations, or after-work gatherings.
- Networking: Building professional relationships through informal means.

4. **Examples**:

- Casual conversations in the break room.
- Text messages between colleagues about project updates.
- Discussions during social events.

Comparison
Importance of Both Forms

- Effective Information Flow: Together, formal and informal communication facilitate a complete flow of information, enabling organizations to operate efficiently.

- Employee Relations: Informal communication helps build relationships, enhance team cohesion, and create a positive work environment.
- Feedback Mechanism: Informal channels provide quick feedback and immediate insights, which can complement formal processes.

Both formal and informal communication play crucial roles in organizations. While formal communication ensures clarity and adherence to policies, informal communication fosters relationships and innovation. Recognizing when to use each type can significantly enhance communication effectiveness and organizational culture.

FIVE

BASICS OF COMMUNICATION (TYPES, CHANNELS AND BARRIERS)

Communication is a fundamental aspect of human interaction, encompassing the processes by which information, thoughts, and feelings are exchanged. Understanding the basics of communication can enhance interpersonal relationships and improve organizational effectiveness. Here are the essential components: types of communication, channels of communication, and barriers to effective communication.

Types of Communication

1. **Verbal Communication**: This involves the use of spoken or written words. It includes face-to-face conversations, telephone calls, video conferences, speeches,

and emails. Verbal communication can be further divided into:

- Oral Communication: Spoken interactions, such as meetings or presentations.
- Written Communication: Text-based interactions, including reports, memos, and messages.

2. **Nonverbal Communication**: This encompasses all forms of communication that do not involve words. It includes body language, facial expressions, gestures, posture, eye contact, and tone of voice. Nonverbal cues often convey emotions and attitudes more powerfully than words.

3. **Visual Communication**: Visuals such as graphs, charts, videos, and images aid in conveying information. This type is often used in presentations, advertising, and educational materials.

4. **Formal Communication**: This follows an established structure or official channels within organizations, such as business reports, policies, and official meetings.

5. **Informal Communication**: Often termed "grapevine" communication, it happens casually and spontaneously among employees or friends. It can foster camaraderie but may sometimes lead to misinformation.

Channels of Communication

Channels refer to the medium through which messages are conveyed. Key channels include:

1. **Face-to-Face**: Direct personal interaction. This is often the most effective channel since it allows for immediate feedback and the interpretation of nonverbal cues.

2. **Telephonic Communication**: Using phones to convey messages. It allows for instant communication but lacks

visual elements.

3. **Written Communication**: Emails, memos, reports, and letters fall under this category. Written channels are useful for documentation and clarity, although they may delay feedback.

4. **Digital Communication**: Includes various forms of electronic messaging like instant messaging, social media, and video conferencing tools. It facilitates rapid communication across distances.

5. **Mass Communication**: Utilizes channels such as television, radio, and online platforms to reach larger audiences. It's often used for marketing, announcements, or public service messages.

Barriers to Effective Communication

Despite the various methods available, several barriers can hinder effective communication:

1. **Physical Barriers**: Environmental factors like noise, distance, or poor infrastructure can interfere with the transmission of messages.

2. **Perceptual Barriers**: Differences in perception or interpretation due to individual experiences, beliefs, and values can lead to misunderstandings.

3. **Language Barriers**: Language differences or jargon can create confusion. Technical terms can alienate those not familiar with them.

4. **Emotional Barriers**: Feelings such as stress, anger, or sadness can impact the clarity of messages. Emotional states may distort how messages are sent, received, and interpreted.

5. **Cultural Barriers**: Variations in cultural backgrounds can lead to differing interpretations and responses to communication. Understanding cultural context is crucial for effective communication across diverse groups.

6. **Technological Barriers**: Issues related to technology, such as software compatibility or lack of access to necessary tools, can prevent effective communication.

Overcoming Barriers to Communication

1. **Active Listening**: Practicing active listening involves giving full attention, showing interest, and providing feedback, ensuring that messages are accurately received.

2. **Simplifying Language**: Using clear and straightforward language can help bridge language gaps and avoid jargon that may confuse others.

3. **Feedback Mechanisms**: Encouraging feedback allows for clarification of misunderstandings and ensures that the messages are interpreted correctly.

4. **Cultural Sensitivity**: Being aware of and respecting cultural differences can minimize misunderstandings and foster better relations among diverse individuals.

5. **Creating a Conducive Environment**: Ensuring a distraction-free environment can improve focus and clarity in communication.

Understanding the types, channels, and barriers of communication is essential for improving personal interactions and organizational efficiency. By being aware of these aspects, individuals can enhance their communication skills, leading to more effective and meaningful exchanges.

SIX
LISTENING SKILLS

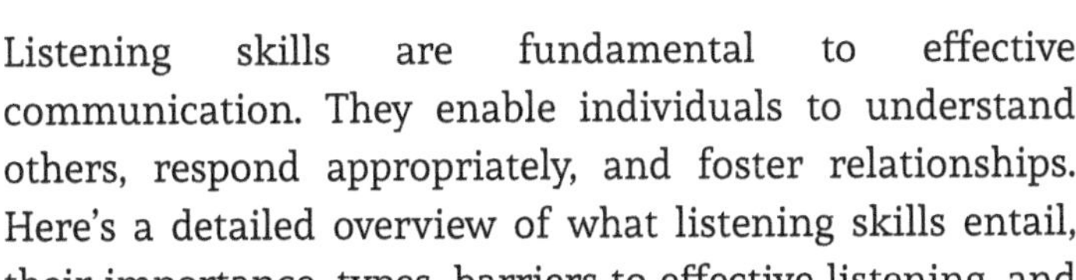

Listening skills are fundamental to effective communication. They enable individuals to understand others, respond appropriately, and foster relationships. Here's a detailed overview of what listening skills entail, their importance, types, barriers to effective listening, and tips for improving them.

What are Listening Skills?

Listening skills refer to the ability to actively understand and interpret spoken language. It encompasses not just hearing the words spoken, but also comprehending the meaning, emotions, and intentions behind them.

Importance of Listening Skills

1. **Enhanced Communication**: Good listening fosters clearer communication and reduces misunderstandings.

2. **Building Relationships**: Active listening builds trust and rapport, making interactions more meaningful and effective.

3. **Problem-Solving**: Listening carefully can provide critical information necessary for resolving conflicts and making informed decisions.

4. **Empathy and Understanding**: Effective listening allow individuals to appreciate different perspectives, cultivating empathy.

5. **Learning and Retention**: Listening enhances learning by ensuring that important information is absorbed and retained.

Types of Listening

1. **Active Listening**: Involves fully engaging with the speaker, showing interest, and providing feedback. Techniques include nodding, maintaining eye contact, and paraphrasing.

2. **Reflective Listening**: Focuses on reflecting back what the speaker has communicated, showing understanding and empathy. It often involves summarizing the speaker's main points.

3. **Critical Listening**: Used when analysing or evaluating the information being presented. This type of listening involves assessing arguments and identifying biases.

4. **Empathetic Listening**: Involves listening to understand the speaker's feelings and emotions. It focuses on experiencing the speaker's perspective without judgment.

5. **Informational Listening**: Aims to gather information and learn. This type of listening is essential in educational and professional settings where comprehension is critical.

Barriers to Effective Listening

1. **Distractions**: Environmental factors such as noise, multitasking, or technological interruptions can hinder listening ability.

2. **Prejudice or Bias**: Personal beliefs and biases can prevent open understanding and evaluation of the speaker's message.

3. **Emotional Interference**: Strong emotions like anger or sadness can cloud comprehension and distract from the conversation.

4. **Assumptions**: Making assumptions about the speaker or their message can lead to misunderstanding, as one might respond without fully listening.

5. **Lack of Interest**: Disinterest in the topic or speaker can lead to passive listening or distraction.

Tips for Improving Listening Skills

1. **Pay Attention**: Focus fully on the speaker, avoiding external distractions. Show through body language that you are engaged.

2. **Practice Active Listening**: Use verbal and non-verbal cues (e.g., nodding, saying "I see") to demonstrate you are listening.

3. **Avoid Interrupting**: Allow the speaker to finish their thoughts without interjecting. This shows respect and helps you catch the complete message.

4. **Ask Clarifying Questions**: If something is unclear, ask questions to gain a better understanding. This indicates that you value the conversation.

5. **Paraphrase and Summarize**: Reflect back what you've heard to confirm understanding. This can also provide the speaker an opportunity to clarify.

6. **Practice Mindfulness**: Being present in the moment can enhance focus and reduce distractions, allowing for better listening.

7. **Be Patient**: Allow silence after someone has finished speaking. This can encourage them to elaborate further, enhancing understanding.

8. **Cultivate Empathy**: Try to understand the speaker's perspective and emotions, which can lead to deeper connections.

Listening skills are essential for effective communication in both personal and professional contexts. By understanding the different types of listening, recognizing barriers, and implementing strategies to improve these skills, individuals can significantly enhance their interactions and relationships. Active and empathetic listening fosters a culture of respect, understanding, and collaboration, making it a crucial component of effective communication.

SEVEN

Communication on Social Media Platforms

Communication on social media platforms has transformed how people connect, share information, and express themselves. While it offers numerous benefits, it also presents challenges. Below is an overview of the dynamics of communication on social media, including its advantages, disadvantages, best practices, and tips for effective engagement.

Advantages of Social Media Communication

1. **Accessibility**: Social media platforms are available to a vast audience, allowing users to communicate across geographical boundaries easily.

2. **Instant Interaction**: Users can instantly share information, thoughts, and updates. This immediacy fosters real-time conversations and feedback.

3. **Diverse Formats**: Social media allows for various communication formats—text, images, videos, live streams, and more—catering to different preferences and enhancing engagement.

4. **Community Building**: Social media fosters communities around shared interests, enabling individuals to connect and interact with like-minded people.

5. **Networking Opportunities**: Professionals can use social media to network, share expertise, and maintain relationships that may lead to career opportunities.

6. **Amplified Voice**: Social media provides a platform for marginalized voices and causes, promoting awareness and mobilization around social issues.

Disadvantages of Social Media Communication

1. **Miscommunication**: The absence of non-verbal cues can lead to misunderstandings. Tone and intent can be easily misread in text-based communication.

2. **Overload of Information**: Users can be overwhelmed by the sheer volume of content, making it difficult to discern credible information from noise.

3. **Cyberbullying and Harassment**: Anonymity can embolden negative behaviour, leading to bullying or harassment on the platform.

4. **Privacy Concerns**: Sharing personal information can lead to privacy breaches and data misuse, raising concerns about security.

5. **Echo Chambers**: Social media algorithms can create echo chambers, where users are exposed only to information that reinforces their existing beliefs, limiting exposure to diverse opinions.

6. **Reduced Face-to-Face Interaction**: Heavy reliance on social media can diminish in-person social skills and lead to feelings of isolation.

Best Practices for Communication on Social Media

1. **Be Authentic**: Genuine communication fosters trust and engagement. Share your true thoughts and insights to connect with your audience.

2. **Stay Professional**: For professional accounts, maintain a level of professionalism. Be mindful of language and content that reflects your brand or personal image.

3. **Engage Actively**: Respond to comments and messages promptly. Actively engaging with your audience helps build rapport and community.

4. **Mind Your Tone**: Use appropriate language and tone to match the context of your message. Humor and casual language may not always be suitable.

5. **Fact-Check Information**: Ensure that the information you share is accurate and credible to maintain your credibility and prevent misinformation.

6. **Respect Diversity**: Acknowledge and respect diverse opinions. Engaging in constructive debates can be rewarding but requires sensitivity and open-mindedness.

7. **Use Visuals Wisely**: Incorporate images and videos to enhance your messages. Visual content can capture attention and improve engagement.

8. **Monitor Your Reputation**: Regularly check feedback and comments on your posts to address any negative interactions and uphold a positive reputation.

Tips for Effective Engagement

1. **Know Your Audience**: Tailor your content and communication style to meet the needs and preferences of your audience. Understand their interests and concerns.

2. **Schedule Content**: Plan and schedule your posts to maintain consistency in communication. This helps keep your audience engaged.

3. **Utilize Hashtags**: Using relevant hashtags can increase the visibility of your posts and help you connect with a broader audience.

4. **Share User-Generated Content**: Highlight content created by your audience or followers. This fosters community and encourages participation.

5. **Be Mindful of Timing**: Post at optimal times when your audience is most active. This can lead to higher engagement rates.

6. **Encourage Feedback**: Ask for opinions and feedback from your audience. This shows that you value their input and fosters a collaborative environment.

7. **Stay Informed**: Keep up with trends, platform updates, and changes in user behaviour to adapt your communication strategies effectively.

Communication on social media platforms is a potent tool for connecting individuals and communities. While it presents unique advantages such as accessibility and the ability to share diverse content, it also comes with challenges like miscommunication and privacy risks. By practicing effective communication strategies and actively engaging with audiences, users can harness the full potential of social media while mitigating its drawbacks. Effective communication can lead to stronger relationships, greater awareness, and a richer exchange of ideas in the digital age.

EIGHT

PLANNING AND EXECUTING DIFFERENT TYPES OF MESSAGES

Effective written communication relies on planning and executing various types of messages tailored to their purpose and audience. Here's a guide to help you understand the process for different types of messages: formal letters, emails, and informal communications.

1. Planning Messages

a. **Identify the Purpose**:

- Determine the main goal of your message:
- Informing: Are you sharing information or updates?
- Requesting: Are you asking for assistance or information?
- Persuading: Are you trying to convince someone of a viewpoint?

- Apologizing: Are you addressing a mistake or misunderstanding?

b. **Analyze Your Audience**:

- Understand who will read your message:
- Consider their familiarity with the topic.
- Adjust the tone and complexity of your language based on their relationship to you (superior, peer, friend).

c. **Gather Information**:

- Compile all necessary facts, figures, and context to support your message.
- Consider potential questions the recipient may have and prepare responses.

d. **Organize Your Thoughts**:

- Create an outline to structure your message logically.
- Decide on key points and examples that will effectively convey your message.

2. Types of Written Messages
a. **Formal Letters**
Layout:

- Header: Your address, date, recipient's address.
- Salutation: Use formal greetings (e.g., "Dear Mr./Ms. [Last Name]").
- Body: Divide into paragraphs (introduction, main content, conclusion).

- Closing: Formal closing phrases (e.g., "Sincerely," "Yours faithfully").
- Signature: Include your name and title.

Execution:

- Use professional and clear language.
- Be concise while providing sufficient detail.
- Proofread for spelling and grammar to maintain professionalism.

b. **Emails**
Layout:

- Subject Line: A clear and relevant subject summarizing the email's purpose.
- Greeting: Appropriate formality based on the recipient (e.g., "Hi" for colleagues, "Dear" for superiors).
- Body: Short paragraphs or bullet points to enhance readability.
- Closing: Simple sign-off (e.g., "Best regards," "Thank you").
- Signature: Your name, title, and contact information.

Execution:

- Maintain a professional yet approachable tone.
- Address the recipient's needs in the introduction.
- Keep the content focused and actionable.
- Use clear calls to action if expecting a response or next steps.

c. **Informal Messages**

Layout:

- Greeting: Casual and friendly (e.g., "Hey," "Hi").
- Body: Use a conversational tone; no need for formal structure.
- Closing: Friendly sign-offs (e.g., "Cheers," "Talk soon").

Execution:

- Personalize the message based on your relationship with the recipient.
- Feel free to use humour or casual expressions if appropriate.
- Keep it brief but engaging, incorporating multimedia if desired (e.g., emoji, images).

3. Executing Your Message
a. **Choose the Right Medium**:

- Decide whether to use email, formal letters, chat, or social media based on context and preference.

b. **Revise and Edit**:

- Review your message for clarity, tone, and purpose.
- Make revisions to enhance fluidity and coherence.

c. **Timing and Follow-Up**:

- Send your message at an appropriate time considering the recipient's schedule.
- If necessary, follow up to ensure the message was received and understood.

4. Best Practices for All Types of Messages

- Be Clear and Concise: Make your points without unnecessary detail.
- Maintain Professionalism: Always consider how the recipient may interpret your words.
- Tailor Your Style: Adjust your voice and tone based on the context and audience.
- Proofread: Check for errors in spelling, grammar, and punctuation before sending.

Planning and executing different types of written messages is essential for effective communication. By understanding the purpose, audience, and appropriate format, you can craft messages that resonate and achieve your communication goals. Whether it's a formal letter, an email, or an informal message, thoughtful planning and careful execution will enhance clarity and engagement.

NINE
EMAILS

Emails are a crucial component of written communication, especially in professional settings. They serve several functions, including conveying information, facilitating conversations, and managing relationships. Here's an overview of their role, structure, best practices, and common pitfalls.

Role of Emails in Written Communication

1. **Formal Communication**: Emails provide a formal means to communicate, often serving as a written record of conversations and decisions.

2. **Accessibility**: They enable communication across different time zones and locations, allowing recipients to respond at their convenience.

3. **Efficiency**: Emails can convey complex information quickly and can be distributed to multiple recipients with minimal effort.

4. **Documentation**: They serve as documentation for agreements, transactions, or discussions, which can be referred to later if needed.

5. **Tone and Professionalism**: The tone of an email can reflect the professionalism of the sender and organization,

impacting relationships and perceptions.

Structure of an Email

1. **Subject Line**: A clear and concise subject line helps the recipient understand the email's purpose at a glance.

2. **Greeting/Salutation**: This sets the tone and establishes rapport. Using the recipient's name adds a personal touch.

3. **Body**: The content should be organized logically:

- Introduction: Briefly state the purpose of the email.
- Main Content: This may include background information, requests, or explanations.
- Conclusion: Summarize key points or outline next steps.

4. **Closing**: Conclude the message with a polite closing statement, such as "Best regards" or "Sincerely."

5. **Signature**: Include your name, title, and contact information to maintain professionalism.

Best Practices for Email Communication

1. **Be Clear and Concise:** Get to the point early. Use short paragraphs and bullet points to enhance readability.

2. **Proofread**: Spelling and grammatical errors can undermine professionalism, so always review emails before sending.

3. **Use Professional Language**: Avoid slang, overly casual expressions, or emojis in professional emails.

4. **Ensure Proper Etiquette**: Use appropriate greetings and closings, and be mindful of recipient titles (Dr., Mr., Ms., etc.).

5. **Respond Promptly**: A timely response indicates professionalism and respect for the recipient's time.

6. **Be Mindful of Tone**: Written communication can be misinterpreted. Use polite language and, when appropriate,

soften requests or directives.

7. **Limit Attachments and CC/BCC Use**: Too many attachments can overwhelm recipients. Share files via secure links if possible. Use CC and BCC judiciously to respect others' privacy.

Common Pitfalls in Email Communication

1. **Overuse of Emails**: Relying exclusively on email for communication can lead to miscommunications. In some cases, a face-to-face meeting or phone call may be more effective.

2. **Neglecting Subject Lines**: A vague or missing subject line can confuse recipients and lead to overlooked emails.

3. **Ignoring the Audience**: Tailor your language and content to the expectations and understanding level of the recipient.

4. **Inappropriate Tone**: Sarcasm or humour can be misinterpreted in written form, so be cautious.

5. **Lack of Follow-Up**: If the email requires action or a response, be sure to follow up as necessary.

6. **Failing to Use Formatting**: Long, unformatted emails can be daunting. Use headlines, bullet points, and paragraphs for easier comprehension.

Emails are a vital means of written communication, especially in professional contexts. When constructed thoughtfully, they can facilitate effective communication, strengthen relationships, and enhance clarity. By adhering to best practices and avoiding common pitfalls, individuals can improve their email communication skills significantly.

TEN

FORMAL LETTERS (PLANNING & LAYOUT OF BUSINESS LETTER)

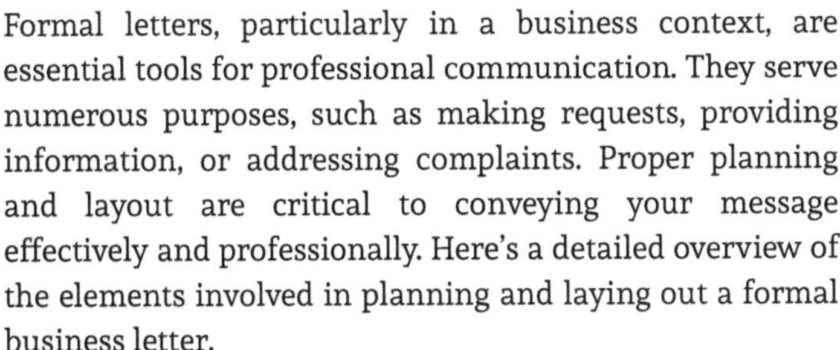

Formal letters, particularly in a business context, are essential tools for professional communication. They serve numerous purposes, such as making requests, providing information, or addressing complaints. Proper planning and layout are critical to conveying your message effectively and professionally. Here's a detailed overview of the elements involved in planning and laying out a formal business letter.

Purpose of Formal Letters

- **Documentation**: Formal letters provide a written record of important communications.
- **Professionalism**: They convey a sense of seriousness and respect, demonstrating professionalism.
- **Clarity**: A structured format enhances clarity, making it easier for the recipient to grasp the intent of the letter.

Planning a Formal Letter

- **Identify the Purpose**: Before writing, clarify the purpose of your letter. Are you requesting information, making a complaint, or conveying important news?
- **Know Your Audience**: Tailor your tone and content to your recipient. Consider their role, background, and expectations.
- **Gather Information**: Compile any necessary information or supporting documents that may be needed to strengthen your letter.
- **Outline Main Points**: Create an outline of key points to be included in the letter. This will help maintain focus and coherence.

Layout of a Business Letter

The layout of a formal business letter typically follows a standard format, including the following components:

1. **Sender's Address**:

- Place your address at the top right or the top left of the letter.
- Include your full name, address, city, state, and zip code, but omit your name if using company stationery with this information pre-printed.

2. **Date**:

- Write the date below your address. Use a formal format, such as "October 18, 2023."

3. **Recipient's Address**:

- Below the date, provide the recipient's name, title, company name (if applicable), and address, aligned to the left.

4. **Salutation/Greeting**:

- Begin with "Dear [Title] [Last Name]," using appropriate titles (Mr., Ms., Dr., etc.). If you don't know the name, "Dear Sir/Madam" is acceptable.

5. **Subject Line (optional)**:

- Some letters may include a subject line to clarify the purpose. This is usually placed between the salutation and the body of the letter. For example, "Subject: Request for Information."

6. **Body of the Letter**:

- Introduction: State the purpose of the letter clearly and concisely. Briefly introduce yourself if necessary.
- Main Content: Elaborate on the main points, providing sufficient detail. Use clear and straightforward language.
- Conclusion: Summarize key points, restate requests if needed, and express appreciation for the recipient's time

and consideration.

7. **Closing**:

- Use a formal closing statement such as "Sincerely," "Best regards," or "Yours faithfully." Leave a few lines for your signature.

8. **Signature**:

- After the closing, sign your name in the space provided and type your full name below it. Include your job title and company name if applicable.

9. **Enclosures/Attachments (if applicable)**:

- If you are including additional documents, note this below your signature with "Enclosure" or "Attachment" followed by a list of the included documents.

Best Practices for Writing Formal Letters

- **Be Concise**: Stay focused on the topic. Avoid unnecessary jargon and keep sentences clear and to the point.
- **Use Formal Language**: Maintain a professional tone throughout the letter. Avoid slang or overly casual expressions.
- **Proofread**: Review your letter for spelling and grammatical errors before sending it. A polished letter creates a positive impression.
- **Be Polite**: Use courteous language, especially when making requests or addressing concerns.

- **Format Appropriately**: Use a standard font (like Times New Roman or Arial), 11–12-point size, and adequate spacing for readability.

Formal letters are an integral part of effective written communication in business. By carefully planning content and adhering to a professional layout, you ensure clarity, respect, and professionalism in your correspondence. Incorporating best practices can enhance your communication skills and further the objectives you seek to achieve through your letters.

ELEVEN

INFORMAL MESSAGES ON E-PLATFORMS

Informal messages on e-platforms refer to casual, conversational communications that take place through various digital channels, such as social media, messaging apps, email, and forums. These messages often aim to create a relaxed atmosphere where users can share thoughts, jokes, and personal updates without adhering to the formalities typically found in professional or traditional communications. Here's a breakdown of key aspects of informal messaging on e-platforms:

Characteristics of Informal Messages:

1. **Casual Tone:**

- Informal messages often use a friendly or playful tone, reflecting the relationship between the sender and the recipient.
- Emojis, slang, and informal language are common.

2. **Conciseness**:

- Messages are typically brief and to the point, though they can be longer depending on the context.
- Users often skip punctuation or grammar rules, making the exchange feel more spontaneous.

3. **Multimedia Use**:

- Informal communication often incorporates images, GIFs, stickers, and videos to convey emotion or context.
- These elements enhance engagement and help convey messages more dynamically.

4. **Real-Time Interaction**:

- Many platforms facilitate instant communication, allowing users to respond promptly, which contributes to a conversational flow.
- This immediacy strengthens social bonds and keeps discussions lively.

5. **Personalization**:

- Informal messages often include personal anecdotes, tailored responses, or inside jokes relevant to the audience.
- This level of personalization makes exchanges more relatable and meaningful.

Platforms for Informal Messaging:
1. **Social Media**:

- Platforms like Facebook, Twitter, Instagram, and TikTok allow users to post casual updates, reactions, and messages to friends and followers.
- Conversations can unfold in comments, direct messages, or posts.

2. **Messaging Apps**:

- Apps like WhatsApp, Messenger, Snapchat, and Telegram are designed for real-time conversations.
- Users can share voice notes, photos, videos, and texts in a flexible manner.

3. **Forums and Community Boards**:

- Platforms like Reddit or Discord foster informal discussions among users based on shared interests.
- Members can engage in playful banter and exchange ideas without strict moderation.

Impact of Informal Messaging:
1. **Social Connections**:

- Informal messages enhance friendships and relationships by promoting spontaneity and relaxed communication.
- They often lead to deeper connections as people express their true selves more comfortably.

2. **Cultural Shifts**:

- The rise of informal messaging has shifted social norms around communication, focusing more on authenticity than formality.

- It encourages a more open exchange of thoughts and feelings, breaking down barriers.

3. **Influence on Language**:

- The emergence of informal communication styles has influenced language evolution, leading to the popularization of new words, phrases, and linguistic trends.

4. **Workplace Dynamics**:

- Informal messaging has made its way into professional settings, with tools like Slack and Microsoft Teams allowing team members to communicate more casually.
- While this can foster a relaxed atmosphere, it's essential to maintain some level of professionalism.

Tips for Effective Informal Messaging:
1. Know Your Audience:

- Tailor your tone and content based on who you're messaging to ensure appropriateness and relatability.

2. **Be Mindful of Length**:

- While informality allows leniency, try to avoid overly long messages to keep the conversation engaging and manageable.

3. **Use Emojis Judiciously**:

- Emojis can enhance messages but should be used appropriately to avoid misinterpretation.

4. **Stay Authentic**:

- Authenticity resonates well in informal contexts; feel free to express your true self while being respectful of others.

5. **Respect Boundaries**:

- Be aware of others' comfort levels and preferences regarding informal communication to foster a positive interaction.

Informal messages on e-platforms play a significant role in modern communication, blending casual interaction with multimedia elements to create engaging conversations. By understanding their characteristics, platforms, and impact, individuals can navigate informal messaging effectively, enriching their social interactions in both personal and professional realms.

TWELVE

NEGATIVE MESSAGES: INDIRECT & DIRECT NEGATIVE MESSAGES

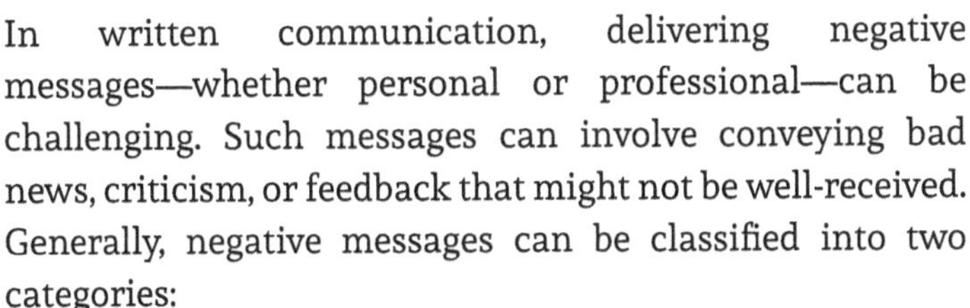

In written communication, delivering negative messages—whether personal or professional—can be challenging. Such messages can involve conveying bad news, criticism, or feedback that might not be well-received. Generally, negative messages can be classified into two categories:

- Direct negative messages
- Indirect negative messages

Here's a breakdown of each type, including their characteristics, when to use them, and tips for crafting them effectively.

Direct Negative Messages
Characteristics:

- Straightforward Approach: Direct negative messages convey the bad news or criticism immediately and without ambiguity.
- Clear Language: The language used is typically simple and direct, leaving no room for misinterpretation.
- Less Context: These messages focus more on the core issue than on cushioning the blow with additional context.

When to Use:

- Urgent Situations: In cases where immediate action is required or the recipient needs to be informed quickly.
- Familiar Relationships: When you have a clear understanding of the recipient's expectations and responses, and a direct approach is acceptable.
- Low-Stakes Contexts: Situations that are less sensitive, where directness can be appreciated, such as minor mistakes.

Example of a Direct Negative Message:
"Your application for the position has not been accepted. We appreciate your interest but will be moving forward with other candidates."

Tips for Crafting Direct Negative Messages:

- **Be Clear and Concise**: Get to the point without unnecessary embellishment.
- **Maintain Professionalism**: Even with a direct approach, maintain a respectful tone.
- **Offer Solutions, If Possible**: If relevant, provide next steps or alternatives.

Indirect Negative Messages
Characteristics:

- **Cushioned Approach**: Indirect negative messages first provide context or positive comments before delivering the bad news, softening the impact.
- **Emphasis on Relationship**: Helps preserve the relationship by showing empathy and consideration for the recipient's feelings.
- **More Narrative**: These messages often include explanations or rationale that leads to the negative conclusion.

When to Use:

- Sensitive Situations: When the subject matter is delicate, such as performance reviews or personal matters.
- Strained Relationships: If past interactions have led to tension, an indirect approach can ease communication.
- High-Stakes Contexts: When the consequences of the news are significant, such as layoffs or major policy changes.

Example of an Indirect Negative Message:
"I want to start by thanking you for your hard work on the project. Your efforts were commendable; however, after

careful consideration, we have decided to go in a different direction for this project. We appreciate your understanding."

Tips for Crafting Indirect Negative Messages:

- **Begin with Positives**: Start with positive feedback or appreciation before transitioning to the bad news.
- **Provide Context**: Explain the reasoning behind the negative message to help the recipient understand.
- **End on a Supportive Note**: Offer encouragement or express your willingness to support the recipient in the future.

Choosing Between Direct and Indirect Negative Messages

The choice between direct and indirect negative messages largely depends on the context and the relationship between the sender and recipient. Here are some factors to consider:

- **Nature of the Relationship**: Consider how well you know the recipient and their likely reaction to directness.
- **Severity of the Message**: Assess how impactful the negative news is and its potential emotional effect on the recipient.
- **Cultural Expectations**: Be aware of cultural norms regarding communication styles. Some cultures prefer directness while others value subtlety.

Both direct and indirect negative messages have their appropriate uses in written communication. Understanding the distinctions between these approaches allows for more effective and considerate communication, especially when conveying news that may be difficult for the recipient to receive. By thoughtfully considering the context and crafting your message with care, you can navigate negative communications with greater ease and compassion.

THIRTEEN
PERSUASIVE MESSAGES

In written communication, persuasive messages aim to convince the reader to adopt a specific viewpoint, take action, or agree with a particular idea. Whether it's an email, a proposal, a marketing piece, or a social media post, mastering the art of persuasion is crucial for effectively influencing others. Here's an overview of persuasive messages, including their elements, types, strategies, and tips for effective crafting.

Elements of Persuasive Messages

1. **Clear Purpose**: The primary goal is clearly defined and focused, whether it's to persuade, motivate, or call to action.

2. **Understanding the Audience**: Knowing the audience's needs, interests, and concerns helps tailor the message effectively.

3. **Compelling Evidence**: Use facts, statistics, anecdotes, and examples to support your claims, building credibility and trust.

4. **Emotional Appeal**: Engaging the reader's emotions can enhance persuasion. This may include storytelling that

resonates on a personal level.

5. **Call to Action**: Conclude with a strong and clear call to action (CTA), telling the reader exactly what you want them to do next.

Types of Persuasive Messages

1. **Sales Proposals**: Often used in business settings to promote products or services.

2. **Donor Appeals**: Written requests to solicit funds or support for charities or non-profit causes.

3. **Cover Letters**: Job applications where professionals try to convince hiring managers of their qualifications.

4. **Advocacy Letters**: Communications aimed at promoting a cause, policy change or social issue.

5. **Marketing Content**: Advertisements and promotional materials designed to persuade consumers to buy.

Strategies for Writing Persuasive Messages

1. **Know Your Audience**:

- Identify the audience's demographics, interests, and pain points.
- Tailor your language and arguments to resonate with their values and beliefs.

2. **Establish Credibility**:

- Use credible sources and cite references to build trust.
- Share your qualifications or experiences related to the subject matter.

3. **Use the "AIDA" Model**:

- Attention: Grab the reader's attention with an engaging opener.

- Interest: Create interest with relatable content or intriguing facts.
- Desire: Foster a desire by highlighting benefits and solutions.
- Action: Prompt the reader to take a specific action.

4. **Anticipate Objections**:

- Acknowledge potential counterarguments or objections and address them proactively within the message.
- Offer rebuttals or alternatives that alleviate their concerns.

5. **Use Persuasive Language**:

- Employ powerful and active verbs to convey urgency and impact.
- Use rhetorical questions to engage the reader and provoke thought.

6. **Incorporate Testimonials**:

- Personal stories or testimonials from satisfied clients or users can bolster your claims and make your message relatable.

7. **Appeal to Emotions**:

- Use evocative language to elicit feelings such as joy, fear, or urgency to motivate action.

8. **Visual Elements**:

- Incorporating visuals, such as charts, infographics, or images, can enhance engagement and understanding.

Tips for Crafting Effective Persuasive Messages

1. **Be Concise**: Keep your message clear and to the point. Avoid unnecessary jargon or filler words.

2. **Proofread**: Errors can undermine your credibility. Ensure your writing is free of grammatical and spelling mistakes.

3. **Format for Readability**: Use headings, bullet points, and white spaces to make the message easy to digest.

4. **Practice Empathy**: Show that you understand the reader's perspectives or concerns, fostering a connection.

5. **Follow Up**: If relevant, consider following up with the reader to reinforce your message and encourage action.

Crafting effective persuasive messages requires an understanding of the audience and the art of argumentation. By employing strategies that nurture credibility, emotional appeal, and clear calls to action, you can enhance your ability to persuade in various contexts. Whether you're writing a sales email, a proposal, or an advocacy piece, thoughtful communication can lead to positive results and influence decisions.

FOURTEEN

REQUEST LETTERS TO VARIOUS STAKEHOLDERS

Request letters are a fundamental part of business communication, used to ask stakeholders for specific actions, information, approvals, or resources. These letters can vary in purpose, tone, and style depending on the recipient and the nature of the request. Here's a guide on how to craft effective request letters to various stakeholders, along with examples for clarity.

Structure of a Request Letter

1. **Your Information**: Include your name, title, company name, address, phone number, and email at the top.

2. **Date**: Provide the date on which the letter is being sent.

3. **Recipient's Information**: Include the recipient's name, title, company name, and address.

4. **Salutation**: Use a professional greeting, such as "Dear [Recipient's Name],".

5. **Introduction**: Begin with a brief introduction of yourself or your organization, followed by the purpose of your letter.

6. **Body**: Clearly state your request, providing necessary details. Explain why the request is important and how it will benefit the recipient or their organization.

7. **Conclusion**: Reiterate your request and express gratitude for their consideration. Include a call to action or the next steps.

8. **Closing**: Use a professional closing, such as "Sincerely," followed by your signature and printed name.

Types of Request Letters and Examples

1. **Requesting Information**

Example:

Subject: Request for Market Research Data

Dear [Recipient's Name],

I hope this message finds you well. My name is [Your Name], and I am [Your Position] at [Your Company]. We are currently conducting market research to better understand consumer preferences within the [specific industry or market].

I kindly request any available data or reports related to your recent market analysis. This information would greatly assist us in refining our strategy and ensuring we align with market trends.

Thank you for considering my request. I appreciate any assistance you can provide and look forward to your prompt response.

Sincerely,

[Your Name]

[Your Position]

[Your Company]

---

2. **Requesting Approval**
Example:
Subject: Request for Approval of Marketing Budget
Dear [Recipient's Name],

I hope you are doing well. I am writing to seek your approval for the proposed marketing budget for the upcoming quarter. As you know, we aim to increase our outreach and enhance brand visibility.

Attached to this letter is a detailed breakdown of the budget, along with projected outcomes and potential ROI. I believe this investment will significantly contribute to our growth objectives.

Please review the proposal at your earliest convenience, and let me know if you require any additional information.

Thank you for your consideration.

Best regards,
[Your Name]
[Your Position]
[Your Company]

---

3. **Requesting a Meeting**
Example:
Subject: Request for a Meeting to Discuss Project Collaboration

Dear [Recipient's Name],

I hope this note finds you in good spirits. I am [Your Name], the [Your Position] at [Your Company], and I am reaching out to propose a meeting to discuss potential collaboration on our upcoming project, [Project Name].

I believe our companies share common goals, and collaborating could yield significant benefits for both parties. I would appreciate the opportunity to explore this further.

Could you please let me know your availability next week? I am happy to accommodate your schedule.

Thank you for considering this request. I look forward to your reply.

Warm regards,
[Your Name]
[Your Position]
[Your Company]

---

4. Requesting Resources or Assistance
Example:

Subject: Request for Additional Resources for [Project Name]

Dear [Recipient's Name],

I hope this message finds you well. I am writing to request additional resources for our ongoing project, [Project Name]. As we progress, it has become clear that we need [specific resources, e.g., "two additional team members, increased budget," etc.] to meet our deadlines and quality standards.

The additional resources would help us achieve our project goals while maintaining our commitment to excellence. I appreciate your consideration of this request and look forward to discussing this further.

Thank you for your support.

Sincerely,
[Your Name]
[Your Position]
[Your Company]

Tips for Writing Request Letters
1. **Be Clear and Concise**: State your request directly and ensure it is easy to understand.

2. **Be Polite and Professional**: Use courteous language and maintain a professional tone throughout the letter.

3. **Provide Context**: Briefly explain why your request is important and any relevant details to help the recipient understand its significance.

4. **Be Specific**: Clearly outline what you are requesting and any deadlines or specific requirements.

5. **Use Positive Language**: Frame your request positively to encourage a favourable response.

6. **Follow Up**: If you haven't received a response within a reasonable timeframe, consider sending a polite follow-up message.

Request letters are crucial for facilitating communication and achieving objectives in a business context. By following the structure and examples provided, you can effectively communicate your needs to various stakeholders, fostering collaboration and support within your organization and beyond.

FIFTEEN
SALES LETTERS

Sales letters are a crucial component of business communication, serving as a persuasive tool designed to encourage recipients to take specific actions, such as making a purchase, signing up for a service, or attending an event. Effective sales letters combine persuasive writing techniques with a clear understanding of the target audience. Here's a breakdown of what makes a successful sales letter and the elements to include.

Key Components of a Sales Letter

1. **Header**:

- **Company Name and Address**: Promotes brand recognition.
- **Date**: Establishes a timeline for relevance.

2. **Salutation**:

- Use the recipient's name if known (e.g., "Dear Ms. Smith"), as it creates a personal touch.

3. **Opening Paragraph**:

- **Grab Attention**: Start with a strong hook or an intriguing statement.
- **Identify the Need or Problem**: Acknowledge a pain point your audience may have.

4. **Body**:

- **Present the Solution**: Introduce your product or service as the answer to the identified problem.
- **Benefits Over Features**: Highlight the benefits rather than just listing features. Explain how your offering can make life easier, save money, or increase efficiency.
- **Social Proof**: Include testimonials, case studies, or statistics that build credibility.
- **Visual Elements**: Use bullet points, bold text, or images sparingly to enhance readability and draw attention to key points.

5. **Call to Action (CTA)**:

- Clearly state what you want the reader to do next. Whether it's visiting a website, calling for more information, or making a purchase, ensure the CTA is simple and compelling.

6. **Closing**:

- Reaffirm your offer's value and express appreciation for the reader's time. Use a friendly yet professional tone.

7. **Signature**:

- Include your name, title, contact information, and any other relevant information that reinforces your identity.

Tips for Writing Effective Sales Letters

- **Know Your Audience**: Understanding your target demographic is critical. Tailor your message to resonate with their needs, interests, and pain points.
- **Be Clear and Concise**: Avoid jargon and convoluted phrases. Use straightforward language to ensure your message is easily understood. Stay focused on one main idea to prevent overwhelming the reader.
- **Create Urgency**: Encourage immediate action by highlighting limited-time offers or scarcity (e.g., "Only 10 left in stock!").
- **Be Personable**: Use a conversational tone that reflects the brand's personality, which helps to forge a connection with the reader.
- **Edit and Proofread**: Typos and grammatical errors can undermine your credibility. Ensure your letter is polished and professional.

Types of Sales Letters

- **Direct Sales Letters**: These focus solely on selling a specific product or service.
- **Inquiry Sales Letters**: These respond to inquiries made by potential customers, providing detailed information about products/services.
- **Follow-Up Sales Letters**: Sent after an initial contact, these letters aim to prompt receiver action, reminding them of previous conversations or offers.

Sales letters remain integral to effective business communication. When crafted thoughtfully, they can significantly influence buying decisions and foster long-term customer relationships. With clear messaging, a strong understanding of your audience, and persuasive writing techniques, a well-designed sales letter can yield impressive results and drive business success.

SIXTEEN

COMPLAINT AND FOLLOW-UP LETTERS

Complaint and follow-up letters are essential tools in business communication that facilitate the resolution of issues and maintain a strong relationship between customers and businesses. While complaint letters articulate concerns, follow-up letters ensure that these issues are addressed timely and satisfactorily. Here's a detailed overview of both types of letters, including their structure, purpose, and essential tips for effectiveness.

Complaint Letters

Purpose: A complaint letter serves to formally communicate dissatisfaction with a product, service, or experience. It aims to bring attention to a problem, seek resolution, and often provide feedback for improvement.

Key Components

1. **Header:**

- Include your name, address, email, and phone number at the top.
- Add the date.
- Optionally, include the recipient's name and address.

2. **Salutation**:

- Use a formal greeting, e.g., "Dear [Name/Title]".

3. **Introduction**:

- Begin by stating the purpose of your letter. Mention the product or service and when you purchased or received it.

4. **Details of the Complaint**:

- Clearly and objectively outline the issue.
- Include factual details such as order numbers, receipt copies, and specific incidents.
- Avoid overly emotional language; focus on the facts to enhance credibility.

5. **Express Your Expectations**:

- State what resolution you are seeking (refund, exchange, service correction, etc.).
- Be reasonable and polite in your request.

6. **Closing**:

- Thank the recipient in advance for their attention to the matter.

- Indicate willingness to provide further information if needed.

7. **Signature**:

- Include your name, and if sending a physical letter, sign above your printed name.

Example Structure for a Complaint Letter
[Your Name]
[Your Address]
[City, State, Zip Code]
[Email]
[Phone Number]
[Date]
[Recipient's Name]
[Company Name]
[Company Address]
[City, State, Zip Code]
Dear [Recipient's Name],

I am writing to formally express my dissatisfaction regarding [product/service] that I purchased on [date]. Unfortunately, [describe the issue clearly and concisely].

Given these circumstances, I would appreciate [state your desired outcome].

Thank you for your attention to the matter. I look forward to your prompt response.

Sincerely,
[Your Name]

Tips for Writing Effective Complaint Letters

- **Be Clear and Concise**: Focus on one issue to avoid confusion and ensure your message is understood.

- **Stay Professional**: Keep your tone respectful to foster a cooperative spirit.
- **Provide Documentation**: Attach copies of receipts, warranty information, or previous correspondence to support your case.

Follow-up letters

Purpose: Follow-up letters serve to reiterate concerns raised in complaint letters, express appreciation for resolutions, or remind the recipient of unresolved issues. They are crucial in ensuring communication continues and issues are tracked.

Key Components

1. **Header**:

- Similar to the complaint letter.

2. **Salutation**:

- Use a formal greeting.

3. **Reference Previous Correspondence**:

- Mention your previous complaint or interaction to provide context.

4. **Update on the Situation**:

- Describe any responses received, or lack thereof. State whether the problem has been resolved or if further action is needed.

5. **Restate Your Position**:

- If the issue remains unresolved, clearly restate your request and reinforce your desire for action.

6. **Closing**:

- Thank the recipient for any previous assistance and express anticipation for a resolution.

7. **Signature**:

- Include your name and details.

Example Structure for a Follow-Up Letter
[Your Name]
[Your Address]
[City, State, Zip Code]
[Email]
[Phone Number]
[Date]
[Recipient's Name]
[Company Name]
[Company Address]
[City, State, Zip Code]
Dear [Recipient's Name],
I am writing to follow up on my complaint dated [date of original complaint] regarding [briefly summarize the issue]. I appreciate your initial response, but [describe the current status or lack of response].

To resolve this matter, I would appreciate your prompt attention in [restate your desired outcome].

Thank you for your continued assistance. I look forward to your reply.

Sincerely,

[Your Name]

Tips for Writing Effective Follow-Up Letters

- **Be Courteous**: Express appreciation for any previous communication, even if the outcome was unsatisfactory.
- **Be Persistent, Yet Polite**: If the issue remains unresolved, gentle persistence reinforces your commitment to resolution.
- **Maintain Professionalism**: Regardless of your frustration, professionalism helps keep communication open.

Complaint and follow-up letters are vital in maintaining effective communication and ensuring customer satisfaction. They provide a structured way to articulate grievances and monitor resolutions. By employing clear, respectful language and adhering to professional standards, these letters can facilitate positive outcomes and enhance relationships between businesses and their customers.

SEVENTEEN

PROMOTION LETTERS

Promotion letters are formal documents used in business communication to communicate an employee's promotion within an organization. They serve several purposes, including announcing the promotion, outlining the new role and responsibilities, and expressing appreciation for the employee's contributions. Here's a breakdown of key elements, best practices, and examples of promotion letters to help you understand their importance and structure.

Key Elements of a Promotion Letter

1. **Header**:

- Company Logo (if applicable)
- Company Name
- Address
- Date

2. **Recipient Information**:

- Employee's Name

- Employee's Job Title
- Employee's Address

3. **Subject Line**:

- A brief statement such as "Promotion Announcement."

4. **Salutation**:

- Begin with a formal greeting, e.g., "Dear [Employee's Name],"

5. **Opening Paragraph**:

- State the purpose of the letter upfront, which is to announce the employee's promotion.

6. **Details of the Promotion**:

- Clearly state the new title and the effective date of the promotion.
- Outline the new responsibilities and expectations associated with the role.

7. **Recognition and Appreciation**:

- Acknowledge the employee's contributions, achievements, and qualities that led to the promotion.

8. **Future Goals**:

- Mention any future objectives or goals for the employee in their new role.

9. **Closing**:

- Offer congratulations and express optimism for future success.
- Provide information about the next steps, if any.

10. **Signature**:

- Sign off with a professional closing, such as "Sincerely," followed by the sender's name, job title, and contact information.

Best Practices
1. **Be Clear and Concise**:

- Use straightforward language and avoid complex jargon.

2. **Use a Professional Tone**:

- Maintain professionalism throughout the letter, even if you have a casual relationship with the employee.

3. **Focus on Achievements**:

- Highlight specific examples of the employee's contributions to justify the promotion.

4. **Be Positive**:

- Emphasize the positive aspects of the promotion and the employee's potential.

5. **Proofread**:

- Ensure the letter is free of grammatical and typographical errors before sending.

Sample Promotion Letter

[Company Logo]
ABC Corporation
123 Business Rd.
Business City, ST 12345
Date: [Insert Date]
[Employee's Name]
[Employee's Job Title]
[Employee's Address]
Subject: Promotion Announcement
Dear [Employee's Name],

I am pleased to announce your promotion to the position of [New Job Title], effective [Effective Date]. This decision reflects our recognition of your hard work, dedication, and significant contributions to ABC Corporation.

In your new role, you will be responsible for [list new responsibilities—e.g., leading a team, managing projects, developing strategies, etc.]. We are confident that your skills and experience will contribute greatly to our continued success.

Your performance in your previous role has been exemplary, particularly your achievements in [specific projects or sales targets], demonstrating your ability to [mention key skills or qualities, e.g., leadership, teamwork, innovation].

Looking forward, we expect you to [mention any future goals tied to the new position]. We believe you will thrive in this new capacity and further elevate the standards of excellence at ABC Corporation.

Congratulations on this well-deserved promotion! If you have any questions or need additional details regarding your new position, please do not hesitate to reach out.

Best regards,

[Your Name]

[Your Job Title]

ABC Corporation

[Your Contact Information]

Promotion letters are an important aspect of business communication, recognizing employees for their hard work and dedication while outlining their new roles and expectations. By following a structured approach and using clear language, organizations can ensure that these letters are effective and meaningful. A well-written promotion letter not only boosts employee morale but also reinforces the values and goals of the organization.

EIGHTEEN

JOB APPLICATION LETTERS

Job application letters, often referred to as cover letters, are essential components of the job application process. They accompany a resume and serve as a personal introduction to the potential employer, highlighting the applicant's qualifications, experiences, and enthusiasm for the position sought. Here's an overview to help you understand the purpose, components, best practices, and examples of effective job application letters.

Purpose of a Job Application Letter

1. **Introduction:**

- Introduce the applicant to the employer and explain the purpose of the application.

2. **Highlight Qualifications:**

- Summarize relevant skills and experiences that align with the job description.

3. **Show Enthusiasm**:

- Convey genuine interest in the position and the company.

4. **Encourage Follow-Up**:

- Prompt employers to review the attached resume and consider the applicant for an interview.

Key Components of a Job Application Letter
1. **Header**:

- Applicant's Name
- Address
- Phone Number
- Email Address
- Date
- Employer's Name (if known)
- Company Name
- Company Address

2. **Salutation**:

- Use a formal greeting, such as "Dear [Hiring Manager's Name]," or "Dear Hiring Committee," if the specific name is unknown.

3. **Opening Paragraph**:

- State the position being applied for and where the job was found. Include a brief introduction to who you are.

4. Middle Paragraph(s):

- Elaborate on qualifications, experiences, and skills. Use specific examples to demonstrate how your background fits the role.

5. Closing Paragraph:

- Reiterate interest in the position, express a desire for an interview, and thank the employer for considering your application.

6. Signature:

- Use a professional closing, such as "Sincerely," followed by your name. If sending electronically, you can include a digital signature.

Best Practices for Writing Job Application Letters
1. Tailor Each Letter:

- Customize each letter for the specific position and company. Highlight experiences relevant to the job description.

2. Be Concise:

- Keep the letter to one page and use clear, concise language. Aim for a balance between professionalism and readability.

3. Use Action Words:

- Incorporate strong action verbs to convey enthusiasm and competence, e.g., "managed," "developed," "led."

4. **Proofread**:

- Check for grammatical and spelling errors. A polished letter reflects attention to detail.

5. **Format Professionally**:

- Use a professional font and format the letter properly for easy reading.

Sample Job Application Letter
[Your Name]
[Your Address]
[Your City, State, Zip]
[Your Phone Number]
[Your Email Address]
Date: [Insert Date]
[Employer's Name]
[Company Name]
[Company Address]
[Company City, State, Zip]
Dear [Hiring Manager's Name],

I am writing to express my interest in the [Job Title] position listed on [where you found the job posting]. With a background in [your field or area of expertise], along with [number] years of experience in [specific relevant experiences], I believe I am an excellent fit for your team at [Company Name].

In my previous role at [Your Last Company], I successfully [mention a particularly relevant responsibility or achievement]. This experience equipped me with a strong skill set in [relevant skills], which I believe would be beneficial for the [Job Title] position. I am particularly drawn to this role because [mention why you are interested in this position or company].

Furthermore, I have a proven track record in [another relevant skill or accomplishment]. For instance, [provide a specific example or achievement that relates to the job description]. This experience taught me the importance of [mention any values or skills related to the role].

I am excited about the possibility of contributing to [Company Name] and the opportunity to bring my expertise in [your skills or field] to your esteemed team. Thank you for considering my application. I look forward to the opportunity to discuss my application with you further.

Sincerely,

[Your Name]

Job application letters are pivotal in making a strong first impression on potential employers. A well-crafted letter demonstrates professionalism, attention to detail, and genuine interest in the job and organization. By following the outlined components and best practices, applicants can effectively communicate their qualifications and enthusiasm, increasing their chances of landing an interview and, ultimately, the job.

NINETEEN

COVER LETTERS

Cover letters play a crucial role in business communication, particularly in the job application process. These letters serve as a personal introduction to prospective employers, providing a platform for candidates to present their qualifications, share their enthusiasm for a specific position, and explain why they are a good fit for the organization. Here's a closer look at the nature, importance, structure, writing tips, and examples of effective cover letters.

Importance of Cover Letters

1. Personalization:

- Cover letters allow candidates to personalize their application, demonstrating a connection to the company and the specific position.

2. Highlight Qualifications:

- They give applicants the chance to elaborate on their resume, emphasizing skills and experiences directly related to the job.

3. **Demonstrate Interest:**

- A well-crafted cover letter shows genuine interest in the position and the organization, which can set a candidate apart from the competition.

4. **Provide Context:**

- Candidates can explain gaps in employment, career transitions, or any unique circumstances that may need clarification.

5. **Call to Action:**

- It encourages employers to consider the applicant for an interview, making it a persuasive tool in the application process.

Structure of a Cover Letter
1. Header:

- Your Name
- Your Address
- Phone Number
- Email Address
- Date
- Employer's Name (if known)
- Company Name
- Company Address

2. Salutation:

- Use a formal greeting such as "Dear [Hiring Manager's Name]," or "Dear Hiring Committee," if the specific name is unknown.

3. **Opening Paragraph**:

- Introduce yourself and state the position you are applying for. Briefly mention where you found the job posting.

4. **Middle Paragraph(s)**:

- Elaborate on your qualifications. Highlight specific achievements, skills, or experiences relevant to the job. Use concrete examples to illustrate your fit for the role.

5. **Closing Paragraph**:

- Reiterate your interest in the position, express gratitude for the opportunity to apply, and indicate your desire for an interview.

6. **Signature**:

- Conclude with a professional closing such as "Sincerely," followed by your name.

Tips for Writing an Effective Cover Letter
1. **Tailor Your Letter**:

- Customize each cover letter to reflect the specific job and company. Use keywords from the job description to align your skills.

2. **Be Concise**:

- Keep your letter to one page. Be direct and focus on your most compelling qualifications without unnecessary filler.

3. **Use Professional Language**:

- Maintain a formal tone, using clear and professional language. Avoid slang or overly casual phrasing.

4. **Show Enthusiasm**:

- Clearly convey your excitement about the role and the company. Genuine enthusiasm can make a significant impact.

5. **Edit and Proofread**:

- Review your letter for spelling and grammatical errors. A polished letter reflects professionalism.

Sample Cover Letter
[Your Name]
[Your Address]
[Your City, State, Zip]
[Your Phone Number]
[Your Email Address]
Date: [Insert Date]
[Employer's Name]
[Company Name]
[Company Address]
[Company City, State, Zip]

Dear [Hiring Manager's Name],

I am writing to express my interest in the [Job Title] position as advertised on [where you found the job posting]. With a background in [your field or area of expertise] and [number] years of experience in [specific relevant experiences], I am excited about the opportunity to contribute to your team at [Company Name].

In my previous role at [Your Last Company], I [briefly describe a relevant responsibility or achievement]. This experience helped me develop [specific skills] that I believe will be advantageous for the [Job Title] position you are offering. I am particularly drawn to [Company Name] because of [mention what attracts you to the company or its values].

I also bring experience in [another relevant skill or accomplishment]. For example, [provide a specific achievement or project that showcases your abilities]. This not only demonstrates my capability but also aligns with your team's goals.

I am enthusiastic about the possibility of contributing to [Company Name] and its mission. Thank you for considering my application. I look forward to the opportunity to discuss how my background fits the needs of your team.

Sincerely,

[Your Name]

Cover letters are an integral part of the job application process, providing candidates the chance to present their qualifications in a personal and engaging manner. By following the outlined structure, employing best practices, and tailoring each letter to specific job openings, applicants can effectively communicate their suitability for roles and increase their chances of securing interviews. A strong cover letter can make a lasting impression, setting the stage for successful career opportunities.

TWENTY
RESUME

In written business communication, a "resume" refers to a formal document that summarizes an individual's professional background, skills, experiences, and education. Its primary purpose is to highlight qualifications relevant to a specific job or opportunity. Here are key elements and tips for creating an effective resume in a business context:

Key Elements of a Resume

1. **Contact Information:**

- Include your name, phone number, email address, and LinkedIn profile (if applicable).
- Ensure this information is clear and easy to find at the top of the document.

2. **Objective or Summary Statement:**

- A brief statement (1-2 sentences) summarizing your career goals and what you bring to the position.
- Tailor this section for each application to reflect the job and company values.

3. **Work Experience**:

- List jobs in reverse chronological order, starting with your most recent position.
- Include the title, company name, location, and dates of employment.
- Use bullet points to describe your responsibilities and accomplishments, emphasizing results and metrics when possible (e.g., "Increased sales by 20% in one year").

4. **Education**:

- Include your highest degree first, followed by relevant certifications or training.
- Provide the name of the institution, degree obtained, and graduation date.

5. **Skills**:

- Highlight relevant skills that match the job description (e.g., software proficiency, language fluency, technical skills).
- Consider separating hard skills (technical) from soft skills (interpersonal).

6. **Additional Sections (if applicable)**:

- **Certifications**: Relevant certifications that enhance your qualifications.
- **Volunteer Experience**: Highlight any relevant volunteer work that demonstrates skills or commitment.

- **Awards and Honors**: Mention any professional recognition that adds value to your candidacy.

7. **References**:

- Typically, references are available upon request.
- Optionally, you can state that references are available to maintain professionalism.

Formatting Tips

- **Length**: Keep it concise, ideally one page for early career professionals and two pages for those with extensive experience.
- **Font and Layout**: Use a clear, professional font (e.g., Arial, Calibri) and maintain consistent formatting throughout.
- **Bullet Points**: Use bullet points for readability, especially in experiences and achievements.
- **Active Language**: Start sentences with strong action verbs (e.g., "Developed," "Managed," "Led").
- **Consistent Tense**: Use past tense for previous jobs and present tense for current positions.

Tailoring Your Resume

- **Keyword Optimization**: Use keywords from the job description to pass through Applicant Tracking Systems (ATS).
- **Tailor Content**: Modify your experiences and skills based on the specific role and company culture.

Common Mistakes to Avoid

1. **Typos and Grammar Errors**: Proofread multiple times or have someone else review it.

2. **Lack of Specificity**: Avoid vague statements; be specific about achievements and responsibilities.

3. **Irrelevant Information**: Focus on content that showcases your qualifications for the specific job.

4. **Inconsistent Formatting**: Ensure consistent fonts, sizes, and styles throughout the document.

A well-crafted resume is a vital part of your job application. By focusing on clarity, relevance, and professionalism, you can make a strong impression on potential employers. Customize your resume for each application, and ensure it aligns with your professional narrative to effectively showcase your qualifications.

TWENTY-ONE
RESIGNATION LETTER

A resignation letter is a formal document that an employee submits to their employer to inform them of their decision to leave the organization. It serves as a professional courtesy and helps maintain a positive relationship between the employee and the employer. Here's an outline and a sample resignation letter to illustrate how to craft one effectively.

Key Elements of a Resignation Letter

1. Header:

- Your name and contact information
- Date
- Employer's name and company address

2. Salutation:

- Address your immediate supervisor or HR manager, e.g., "Dear [Manager's Name],"

3. **Statement of Resignation**:

- Clearly state your intention to resign and specify your last working day.

4. **Reason for Leaving (Optional)**:

- You may briefly mention your reason for leaving, but this is not mandatory.

5. **Gratitude**:

- Express appreciation for the opportunities you had while working at the company.

6. **Offer of Assistance**:

- Offer to help with the transition process.

7. **Closing**:

- Use a professional closing statement, e.g., "Sincerely," followed by your signature (if sending a hard copy) and your typed name.

Sample Resignation Letter
[Your Name]
[Your Address]
[City, State, Zip Code]
[Email Address]
[Phone Number]
[Date]
[Manager's Name]

[Company's Name]

[Company's Address]

[City, State, Zip Code]

Dear [Manager's Name],

I am writing to formally resign from my position at [Company's Name], effective [Last Working Day, typically two weeks from the date of the letter].

This decision was not easy, as I have appreciated the opportunity to work with a talented team and have learned a great deal during my time here. However, I have decided to pursue an opportunity that aligns more closely with my career goals.

I want to express my gratitude for the support and guidance you have provided me during my tenure. I am particularly thankful for [specific example of support or learning experience]. It has been a valuable part of my professional development.

I am committed to ensuring a smooth transition and will do everything I can to pass on my responsibilities and help train my replacement during my remaining time.

Thank you again for the opportunity to be a part of [Company's Name]. I hope to stay in touch, and I wish the company continued success in the future.

Sincerely,

[Your Signature (if hard copy)]

[Your Typed Name]

Tips for Writing a Resignation Letter

- **Keep it Professional**: Maintain a positive and professional tone throughout the letter.
- **Be Concise**: Stick to the point and keep the letter brief.
- **Proofread**: Check for any grammatical or spelling errors before sending.

- **Submit in Person if Possible**: If circumstances allow, hand your resignation letter to your manager personally.
- **Follow Up**: After submitting your resignation, consider discussing your departure with your supervisor to clarify any details.

A resignation letter not only facilitates a formal exit but also leaves a lasting impression and can contribute to a positive reference in the future.

TWENTY-TWO
TEAM COMMUNICATION

Team communication in interpersonal communication refers to the ways in which team members interact and share information, fostering collaboration and understanding within a group. Here are some key aspects:

- **Clarity**: Clear communication helps prevent misunderstandings. Team members should express ideas, feedback, and expectations clearly.
- **Active Listening**: Team members must actively listen to each other, demonstrating understanding and respect for different perspectives.
- **Feedback**: Constructive feedback promotes growth and improvement. Teams should cultivate a culture where feedback is given and received positively.
- **Non-verbal Communication**: Body language, eye contact, and tone of voice play significant roles in conveying messages. Awareness of these cues is essential.

- **Conflict Resolution**: Disagreements are inevitable. Effective teams address conflicts through open dialogue and compromise, focusing on solutions rather than blame.
- **Trust Building**: Trust among team members enhances communication. Teams should engage in activities that foster relationships and encourage openness.
- **Use of Technology**: Modern teams often rely on digital tools for communication. Leveraging technology effectively can bridge gaps, especially in remote work settings.
- **Regular Meetings**: Scheduling consistent check-ins can help maintain alignment, share updates, and provide a platform for discussion.
- **Goal Alignment**: Clearly defined team goals ensure everyone is on the same page, making communication more purposeful.
- **Cultural Sensitivity**: In diverse teams, being aware of cultural differences can prevent miscommunication and foster inclusivity.

Effective team communication is essential for collaboration, problem-solving, and achieving collective goals in any organization.

TWENTY-THREE

MANAGING COMMUNICATION DURING ONLINE MEETING

Managing communication during online meetings is crucial for facilitating effective interaction and collaboration among participants. Here are key strategies to enhance interpersonal communication in this context:

1. Preparation: Set clear agendas and goals for the meeting to ensure everyone understands the purpose and can prepare accordingly.

2. Technical Setup: Ensure a reliable platform is used, with all participants familiar with the tools, to minimize disruptions and technical issues.

3. Time Management: Start and end meetings on time. Allocate specific time slots for each agenda item to keep discussions focused.

4. Facilitation: Designate a facilitator to guide the meeting, encourage participation, and ensure that everyone has a chance to contribute.

5. Engagement Techniques: Use polls, breakout rooms, or interactive tools to keep participants engaged and facilitate active participation.

6. Clear Communication: Encourage participants to speak clearly and concisely. Remind them to mute when not speaking to reduce background noise.

7. Visual Aids: Use slides, video clips, or shared screens to support discussions and ensure that information is conveyed effectively.

8. Active Listening: Encourage participants to listen actively, summarizing points, asking clarifying questions, and acknowledging others' contributions.

9. Non-verbal Cues: Be mindful of body language and facial expressions, which can still be observed on video, and encourage participants to keep cameras on when possible.

10. Follow-Up: Summarize key points and action items at the end of the meeting. Send a recap email to ensure that everyone is aligned and accountable.

11. Feedback Mechanism: Create a space for participants to give feedback on the meeting format and communication, fostering continuous improvement.

12. Cultural Awareness: Be sensitive to different communication styles and cultural perspectives, facilitating a respectful environment for all participants.

By implementing these strategies, teams can improve interpersonal communication and collaboration during online meetings, leading to more productive outcomes.

TWENTY-FOUR

COMMUNICATION WITH VIRTUAL TEAM

Effective communication with a virtual team is vital for maintaining collaboration and engagement across distances. Here are some essential elements to consider in interpersonal communication for virtual teams:

1. Establish Clear Goals: Clearly define team objectives and expectations to ensure everyone understands their roles and responsibilities.

2. Choose the Right Tools: Utilize suitable communication platforms (e.g., Slack, Microsoft Teams) for messaging, video conferencing, and project management to enhance interaction.

3. Regular Check-ins: Schedule consistent team meetings and one-on-ones to maintain connection, address concerns, and celebrate achievements.

4. Encourage Open Communication: Foster a culture where team members feel comfortable sharing ideas,

feedback, and concerns without fear of judgment.

5. Utilize Video Calls: Whenever possible, use video conferencing to enhance face-to-face interaction, allowing non-verbal cues to enrich communication.

6. Provide Written Documentation: Share meeting notes, guidelines, and resources electronically to ensure that all team members are informed and can refer back to important information.

7. Be Accessible and Responsive: Encourage team members to reach out for help and promptly respond to inquiries, promoting a sense of support and teamwork.

8. Cultural Sensitivity: Acknowledge and respect different cultural backgrounds and communication styles, creating an inclusive environment for all team members.

9. Celebrate Milestones: Recognize individual and team accomplishments to foster camaraderie and keep morale high in a virtual setting.

10. Use Visual Communication: Incorporate visuals like charts, infographics, or shared screens to clarify complex topics and maintain engagement.

11. Encourage Social Interaction: Organize virtual team-building activities or informal gatherings to strengthen relationships and create a sense of community.

12. Solicit Feedback: Regularly ask for input from team members on communication practices and adapt strategies to better meet the team's needs.

By focusing on these aspects, virtual teams can enhance interpersonal communication, leading to greater collaboration, productivity, and a positive work environment.

TWENTY-FIVE

PRESENTATION SKILLS (VERBAL AND NON-VERBAL)

Improving academic writing on the topic of "Presentation Skills (Verbal and Non-Verbal)" within the realm of Interpersonal Communication can be approached through structured guidance. Here are some strategies and tips to enhance your writing:

1. Understand Your Audience

- Analyze the Audience: Before writing, consider who will read your work. Tailoring your writing style and content to your audience's level of understanding and interest is crucial.
- Use Appropriate Terminology: Adjust your vocabulary and complexity based on your audience. Avoid jargon if your audience is not familiar with it, or explain it

thoroughly if necessary.

2. **Organize Your Ideas**

- Outline Structure: Start with a clear outline. Break your paper into sections: introduction, body (including subsections for verbal and non-verbal skills), and conclusion.

  Example Outline:
  1. Introduction to Presentation Skills
  2. Importance of Verbal Communication

- Clarity and articulation
- Tone and volume
- Use of pauses

  3. Importance of Non-Verbal Communication

- Body language
- Eye contact
- Gestures

  4. Interpersonal Communication Context
  5. Tips for Effective Presentations
  6. Conclusion

- Logical Flow: Ensure each section logically leads to the next. Transitions should be smooth to maintain coherence.

3. **Use Clear and Concise Language**

- Be Direct: Use straightforward language. Avoid unnecessary jargon or overly complex sentences that may confuse the reader.
- Active Voice: Favor the active voice over passive voice, as it typically makes writing more engaging and clearer.

4. Incorporate Evidence and Examples

- Support Your Claims: Use research studies, examples, and case studies to back up your arguments about the importance of presentation skills in interpersonal communication.
- Real-World Applications: Provide examples of effective and ineffective presentations, highlighting what was verbal and non-verbal and how they impacted the audience's perception.

5. Illustrate Verbal and Non-Verbal Skills Distinctly

- Verbal Communication: Discuss aspects such as clarity of speech, choice of words, and engagement through questions or interactive elements.
- Non-Verbal Communication: Delve into body language, gestures, facial expressions, and other non-verbal cues that complement or contradict verbal messages.
- Interrelation of Both: Highlight how verbal and non-verbal skills work together to enhance or detract from the message.

6. Incorporate Visual Aids Where Relevant

- Graphs and Charts: If your paper allows for graphical representations, consider including pie charts or graphs that depict data on effective presentations.

- Images or Examples: A picture of a good or bad presentation can illustrate points more effectively than text alone.

7. **Edit and Revise Your Work**

- Multiple Drafts: Don't overwhelm yourself by expecting to get it right in the first draft. Writing is a process; allow time for several revisions.
- Peer Feedback: Share your drafts with peers for feedback. They may provide insights you hadn't considered.
- Professional Language Check: Consider using tools or services that check grammar and style, or enlist a mentor for review.

8. **Conclude Effectively**

- Summarize Key Points: Recap the main ideas discussed without introducing new information.
- Final Thought: End with a powerful statement or call-to-action that emphasizes the importance of mastering presentation skills in interpersonal communication.

9. **Stay Informed on Current Trends**

- Recent Studies and Articles: Regularly read the latest research in communication studies to ensure your writing reflects current thinking and innovations in the field.

Additional Resources

- Books and Articles: Look into academic books and peer-reviewed articles about effective communication and public speaking.
- Workshops and Seminars: Participate in workshops focused on presentation skills. Your experiences can enrich your writing.

By following these tips and techniques, you should be able to craft a compelling and informative academic piece focused on presentation skills in interpersonal communication, making it engaging and educational for your audience.

TWENTY-SIX
POWERPOINT PRESENTATION SKILLS

When discussing "PowerPoint presentation skills" in the context of interpersonal communication, it's important to focus on how these skills enhance effective communication during presentations. Here's a structured approach to convey this topic:

1. **Introduction to PowerPoint Presentation Skills**

- Define the significance of PowerPoint as a tool for enhancing interpersonal communication.
- Mention the growing importance of presentations in both professional and academic settings.

2. **Effective Slide Design**

- Clarity and Simplicity: Use clear fonts, contrasting colors, and minimal text to avoid overwhelming the audience.

- Visual Aids: Incorporate images, graphs, and charts to complement spoken words and enhance understanding.
- Consistent Theme: Maintain a consistent style and layout throughout the presentation for professionalism.

3. **Verbal Communication Skills**

- Articulation and Tone: Speak clearly with appropriate volume and intonation to engage the audience.
- Pacing: Control your speech rate to allow the audience to absorb the information presented on the slides.
- Engagement Techniques: Use questions, anecdotes, or relevant examples to connect with the audience verbally.

4. **Non-Verbal Communication Skills**

- Body Language: Utilize gestures and movements to emphasize points, ensuring they are open and engaging.
- Eye Contact: Maintain eye contact with the audience to build rapport and convey confidence.
- Facial Expressions: Use appropriate expressions to match the content of your presentation and keep the audience engaged.

5. **Interactive Elements**

- Encourage audience participation through Q&A sessions or interactive polls to boost engagement.
- Be responsive to audience feedback both verbally and non-verbally, adjusting your presentation style as necessary.

6. Rehearsal and Preparation

- Practice your presentation multiple times to increase familiarity with content and flow.
- Test the PowerPoint on the equipment you will use to avoid technical glitches during the actual presentation.

7. Overcoming Common Challenges

- Discuss strategies for dealing with nervousness, such as deep breathing or positive visualization.
- Provide tips on handling questions or interruptions during the presentation gracefully.

8. Conclusion

- Summarize key points about the importance of integrating effective PowerPoint presentation skills with interpersonal communication.
- Highlight the benefits, such as improved audience understanding and retention, and greater engagement.

9. Resources and Further Learning

- Suggest books, online courses, and webinars focused on presentation skills and effective communication.

This structured outline provides a comprehensive view of how PowerPoint presentation skills intersect with interpersonal communication, emphasizing both verbal and non-verbal skill sets.

TWENTY-SEVEN
INFOGRAPHICS

Infographics play a pivotal role in interpersonal communication by visually conveying complex information in an accessible and engaging manner. Here's a structured exploration of their significance:

1. Introduction to Infographics

- Define infographics as visual representations of information, data, or knowledge.
- Emphasize their role in enhancing understanding and retention through visual learning.

2. Benefits of Using Infographics in Communication

- Clarity: Simplifies complex concepts, making them easier to understand.
- Engagement: Captures attention better than text-heavy content, stimulating interest.
- Memory Retention: Visual elements help in remembering information longer.

3. Types of Infographics

- Statistical Infographics: Display data and statistics clearly.
- Geographic Infographics: Use maps to convey location-based information.
- Timeline Infographics: Present historical events or processes in chronological order.
- Process Infographics: Outline steps in a procedure or workflow.

4. Design Principles for Effective Infographics

- Simplicity: Avoid clutter; focus on key messages.
- Color Scheme: Use a cohesive color palette that enhances readability and appeal.
- Typography: Choose fonts that are easy to read; ensure contrasts between text and background.
- Hierarchy: Organize information in a way that guides the viewer's eye logically.

5. Using Infographics in Different Contexts

- Business Communication: Presenting data, reports, or project summaries.
- Education: Aiding teachers in delivering lessons and students in understanding topics.
- Marketing: Visually conveying product benefits and statistics to potential customers.

6. Interpersonal Communication Enhancement

- Facilitates Discussion: Infographics can serve as conversation starters in meetings or presentations.

- Clarifies Misunderstandings: Visuals can help clarify concepts that may be misinterpreted in text form.
- Fosters Collaboration: Encourage teamwork in creating infographics, enhancing group dynamics.

7. **Challenges of Infographics in Communication**

- Over-simplification: Risk of losing critical details if the infographic is too simplified.
- Misinterpretation: Inaccurate or misleading visuals can lead to misunderstandings.
- Accessibility: Ensuring infographics are accessible to all audience members, including those with disabilities.

8. **Best Practices for Sharing Infographics**

- Share infographics in presentations, reports, and social media for broader reach.
- Always credit sources to maintain credibility and transparency.

9. **Conclusion**

- Recap the importance of infographics in creating effective interpersonal communication.
- Highlight their capability to bridge the gap between data and understanding.

10. **Resources for Learning and Creating Infographics**

- Recommend online tools (like Canva, Piktochart) for creating infographics.

- Suggest websites and courses that offer design principles and techniques.

This structured exploration of infographics in interpersonal communication highlights their effectiveness as tools for enhancing understanding, engagement, and collaboration.

TWENTY-EIGHT

INTRODUCTION TO CONTEMPORARY ALTERNATIVES (SUCH AS PREZI, VISME, MICROSOFT SWAY, AND ZOHO)

Introduction to Contemporary Alternatives in Interpersonal Communication

As technology evolves, so do the tools available for enhancing interpersonal communication. Traditional methods like PowerPoint presentations are being complemented or replaced by contemporary alternatives that offer dynamic and interactive features. Here's an overview of some popular options: Prezi, Visme, Microsoft Sway, and Zoho.

1. Prezi

- Overview: A cloud-based presentation software that uses a single canvas instead of traditional slides.
- Features:

1) Zooming Interface: Allows users to navigate between topics fluidly, creating a visual journey.

2) Engaging Visuals: Customizable templates and graphics enhance storytelling.

3) Application in Communication: Facilitates presentations that feel more like conversations, encouraging audience engagement.

2. Visme

- Overview: A versatile visual content creation tool used for presentations, infographics, and other visual media.
- Features:

1) Drag-and-Drop Interface:Easily create visually appealing content without design experience.

2) Data Visualization: Integrates charts, graphs, and widgets to present data clearly.

3) Application in Communication: Ideal for sharing complex information, making it accessible and memorable for audiences.

3. Microsoft Sway

- Overview: A digital storytelling app that enables users to create interactive presentations and reports.
- Features:

1) Fluid Layout: Automatically arranges content for optimal viewing on various devices.

2) Integration with Microsoft Suite: Easily incorporates Word documents, Excel data, and multimedia.

3) Application in Communication: Enhances collaboration by allowing team members to contribute and edit presentations in real-time.

4. Zoho Show

- Overview: Part of the Zoho suite, Zoho Show is a cloud-based presentation tool that emphasizes collaboration.
- Features:

1) Real-Time Collaboration: Multiple users can work on a presentation simultaneously.

2) Variety of Templates: Offers numerous pre-designed layouts for easy customization.

3) Application in Communication: Promotes teamwork and collective input, making presentations more comprehensive and aligned.

5. Benefits of Using Contemporary Alternatives

- Interactivity:These tools often include features that allow audience participation, keeping them engaged.
- Flexibility: Presentations can be easily modified and adapted in real time based on audience feedback.
- Accessibility: Cloud-based options enable seamless sharing and access across devices and locations.

6. Challenges and Considerations

- Learning Curve: Familiarizing oneself with new tools can take time and effort.
- Technical Issues: Dependence on internet connectivity and platform reliability.
- Over-Reliance on Technology: Ensuring that the message remains the focus and not just the flashy features.

7. Conclusion

Contemporary alternatives like Prezi, Visme, Microsoft Sway, and Zoho provide innovative solutions for effective interpersonal communication. They enhance engagement, flexibility, and collaboration, making communication more impactful in both personal and professional contexts. As these tools evolve, they will likely continue to shape the way we share and interact with information.

TWENTY-NINE

DIGITAL COMMUNICATION

Digital communication refers to the transmission of information over digital networks, using electronic devices such as computers, smartphones, and tablets. It encompasses various forms, including:

1. **Email**: Messages sent over the internet, allowing for asynchronous communication.

2. **Instant Messaging**: Real-time text communication through apps like WhatsApp, Slack, or Messenger.

3. **Social media**: Platforms like Facebook, Twitter, and Instagram for sharing content and connecting with others.

4. **Video Conferencing**: Virtual meetings using tools like Zoom or Microsoft Teams, enabling face-to-face interactions from different locations.

5. **Blogs and Websites**: Online platforms for sharing information, articles, or personal thoughts.

6. **Mobile Apps**: Applications designed for smartphones and tablets to facilitate communication.

Digital communication has transformed how we interact, offering instant access to information and global connectivity. However, it also raises issues regarding privacy, misinformation, and the digital divide among different populations.

THIRTY

SOCIAL MEDIA AND INDIVIDUAL

Social media has significantly impacted individuals, influencing various aspects of life including communication, self-expression, and social interaction. Here are some key points on this relationship:

1. Connectivity: Social media allows individuals to connect with friends, family, and new acquaintances across the globe, fostering relationships that may not have been possible otherwise.

2. Self-Expression: Platforms like Facebook, Instagram, and Twitter provide users with a space to share opinions, experiences, photos, and videos, allowing for creative expression and personal branding.

3. Information Sharing: Users can stay informed about news, trends, and interests by following accounts, engaging in discussions, and sharing content.

4. Community Building: Social media fosters communities around shared interests or causes, providing support networks for individuals with similar experiences or challenges.

5. Mental Health Effects: While social media can enhance social connections, it can also contribute to anxiety, depression, and low self-esteem due to comparison, cyberbullying, or negative interactions.

6. Privacy Concerns: Individuals must navigate issues related to personal privacy, including data sharing and the potential for misuse of personal information.

7. Civic Engagement: Social media has become a tool for activism and social change, empowering individuals to raise awareness and mobilize for various causes.

Overall, social media plays a complex role in shaping individual identities and experiences in the digital age.

THIRTY-ONE

SOCIAL MEDIA AND ORGANIZATIONS

Social media has become essential for organizations, transforming how they communicate, market, and engage with stakeholders. Here are some key points regarding the impact of social media on organizations:

1. Brand Awareness: Social media platforms help organizations enhance brand visibility and recognition, reaching a broader audience effectively.

2. Customer Engagement: Organizations use social media to interact with customers, gather feedback, and respond to inquiries, fostering a sense of community and loyalty.

3. Marketing and Advertising: Targeted ads and promotional campaigns on social media allow organizations to reach specific demographics and track engagement metrics, improving marketing strategies.

4. Crisis Management: Organizations can respond quickly to crises or negative publicity on social media, allowing for real-time communication with stakeholders to manage perceptions.

5. Recruitment and Talent Acquisition: Social media platforms like LinkedIn are vital for attracting and recruiting talent, as they provide access to a wider pool of potential candidates.

6. Content Sharing and Thought Leadership: Organizations use social media to share valuable content, showcase expertise, and establish themselves as industry leaders.

7. Market Research: Social media provides insights into customer behavior, preferences, and trends, helping organizations make informed business decisions.

8. Collaboration and Networking: Social media facilitates collaboration among employees and partners, promoting knowledge sharing and innovation.

Overall, social media is a powerful tool for organizations, enhancing communication, marketing, and relationship-building in today's digital landscape.

THIRTY-TWO
MEDIA LITERACY

Media literacy refers to the ability to access, analyze, evaluate, and create media in various forms. It encompasses skills necessary to navigate the complex media environment and promotes critical thinking. Here are key components of media literacy:

1. Access: Understanding how to find and use different media sources and platforms, including traditional (TV, newspapers) and digital (social media, websites).

2. Analysis: Evaluating media messages critically, recognizing techniques used in media to convey messages, and identifying biases or underlying agendas.

3. Evaluation: Judging the credibility and reliability of information sources, discerning between fact, opinion, and misinformation.

4. Creation: Developing the skills to create media content responsibly and ethically, using appropriate tools and formats.

5. Reflection: Considering the impact of media on individuals and society, including effects on behavior, attitudes, and cultural perceptions.

6. Digital Citizenship: Navigating the online world responsibly, understanding issues like privacy, copyright, and digital footprint.

7. Media Influence: Recognizing how media shapes public opinion and influences social norms and behaviors.

Promoting media literacy is essential in empowering individuals to become informed consumers and producers of media, enabling them to engage critically with the content they encounter in everyday life.

THIRTY-THREE
STRONG DIGITAL COMMUNICATION SKILLS

Strong digital communication skills are essential in today's technology-driven environment, facilitating effective interaction across various digital platforms. Here are some key components of these skills:

1. Clarity and Conciseness: Ability to convey messages clearly and directly, minimizing ambiguity to ensure the audience understands the intent.

2. Active Listening: Engaging with the audience by paying attention, asking questions, and responding thoughtfully, whether in virtual meetings or through written communication.

3. Adaptability: Adjusting communication style based on the platform (email, social media, video calls) and the audience, ensuring appropriateness and effectiveness.

4. Technical Proficiency: Familiarity with various digital tools and platforms (e.g., video conferencing, collaboration software, social media) to communicate seamlessly.

5. Professionalism: Maintaining a professional tone, especially in workplace communications, to foster a respectful and productive environment.

6. Emotional Intelligence: Recognizing and responding to emotional cues in digital communication to enhance interpersonal connections and reduce misunderstandings.

7. Feedback and Collaboration: Providing and receiving constructive feedback, facilitating teamwork, and engaging collaboratively in digital spaces.

8. Cultural Awareness: Understanding diverse backgrounds and perspectives to communicate respectfully and inclusively in a global digital landscape.

9. Visual Communication: Using visuals effectively (charts, infographics, videos) to complement messages and enhance understanding.

10. Social Media Savvy: Navigating social media platforms effectively, understanding appropriate content sharing, audience engagement, and brand representation.

Developing strong digital communication skills is crucial for success in professional and personal interactions in the modern world, enabling effective collaboration, relationship-building, and information sharing.

THIRTY-FOUR

EMAIL AND INSTANT MESSAGING

Email and Instant Messaging (IM) are two fundamental modes of digital communication, each with unique characteristics and best practices. Here's a breakdown of both:

Email

1. Formality: Generally more formal than instant messaging. Suitable for professional communication, detailed information sharing, and situations requiring documentation.

2. Structure: Typically includes a subject line, greeting, body, and closing. Clarity and organization in content are essential to facilitate understanding.

3. Subject Lines: Clear and concise subject lines are crucial for guiding recipients on the email's content and urgency.

4. Attachments: Commonly used to send documents, images, or files. Important to ensure attachments are relevant and properly labeled.

5. Response Time: Expect slower responses compared to IM; however, timely replies are still appreciated in professional settings.

6. CC/BCC: Carbon copy (CC) and blind carbon copy (BCC) features allow for group communication while maintaining privacy and relevance.

7. Signature: Include a professional email signature with contact information and company details for credibility.

Instant Messaging (IM)

1. Informality: More casual and informal, often used for quick, real-time communication. Ideal for brief updates, questions, or team collaboration.

2. Real-Time Interaction: Immediate back-and-forth conversations, allowing for quick resolution of queries and spontaneous discussions.

3. Presence Indicators: Many IM platforms show users' availability (online, busy, offline), facilitating real-time engagement.

4. Short Messages: Messages are usually brief and to the point. Emoticons, gifs, and informal language are often acceptable depending on context.

5. Channels/Groups: Options to create group chats for team discussions, enhancing collaboration and information sharing.

6. File Sharing: Easy sharing of files, images, and links within conversations, promoting quicker exchanges without formal attachments.

7. Search Functionality: Allows users to quickly find past messages or shared content within chats, enhancing information retrieval.

Best Practices for Both

- **Clarity**: Be clear and concise in your messaging to avoid misunderstandings.
- **Professionalism**: Maintain professionalism appropriate to the context, especially in emails.
- **Response Etiquette**: Acknowledge messages promptly, whether in email or IM.
- **Proper Use**: Choose the appropriate medium based on the context, urgency, and recipient.

By understanding the distinctions and best practices for email and instant messaging, individuals can communicate effectively and efficiently in a digital landscape.

THIRTY-FIVE

VIDEO CONFERENCING AND E-MEETINGS

Video conferencing and e-meetings are essential components of digital communication, particularly in today's remote work environment. Here are some key aspects:

Benefits:

1. **Real-Time Interaction**: Facilitates immediate communication, enhancing collaboration.

2. **Cost-Effective**: Reduces travel expenses and time associated with in-person meetings.

3. **Global Reach**: Connects teams and clients from different locations easily.

4. **Flexibility**: Allows participants to join from anywhere, accommodating diverse schedules.

Tools:

1. **Zoom**: Popular for its user-friendly interface and features like breakout rooms.

2. **Microsoft Teams**: Integrates with Microsoft Office Suite, ideal for organizations already using those tools.

3. **Google Meet**: Convenient for quick meetings and integration with Google Workspace.

4. **Webex**: Known for its robust security features, often used in enterprise environments.

Best Practices:

1. **Agenda Setting**: Share an agenda ahead of time to keep the meeting focused.

2. **Technical Check**: Ensure all participants test their equipment and internet connection before the meeting.

3. **Engagement**: Encourage participation through questions and polls to maintain attention.

4. **Recording**: Record meetings for those who cannot attend, ensuring everyone stays informed.

Challenges:

1. **Technical Issues**: Connectivity problems can disrupt communication.

2. **Distractions**: Participants may be tempted to multitask, reducing engagement.

3. **Time Zone Differences**: Scheduling can be complex with remote teams in various locations.

Future Trends:

1. **Enhanced AI Integration**: Improved transcription, real-time translation, and smarter scheduling tools.

2. **Greater Virtual Reality Use**: Immersive experiences that mimic in-person interactions.

3. **Hybrid Meetings**: A blend of in-person and virtual participation, catering to diverse work environments.

Incorporating effective video conferencing and e-meeting strategies enhances digital communication, making collaborations seamless and productive.

THIRTY-SIX
DIGITAL COLLABORATION

Digital collaboration refers to the use of digital tools and platforms to work together effectively and efficiently, regardless of physical location. Here's an overview:

Key Components of Digital Collaboration:

1. Communication Tools:

- **Instant Messaging**: Tools like Slack and Microsoft Teams facilitate real-time conversations.
- **Video Conferencing**: Platforms such as Zoom, Google Meet, and Webex enable face-to-face interactions, enhancing communication.

2. Project Management:

- **Task Management Systems**: Tools like Asana, Trello, and Monday.com help teams organize tasks, set deadlines, and assign responsibilities.
- **Document Collaboration**: Google Workspace and Microsoft Office 365 allow multiple users to edit

documents simultaneously.

3. **File Sharing**:

- **Cloud Storage Solutions**: Services such as Google Drive, Dropbox, and OneDrive provide secure storage and easy access to files from anywhere.

4. **Version Control**:

- Tools like Git and GitHub are essential for teams working on software projects, allowing collaboration on code while tracking changes.

5. **Feedback and Review**:

- Utilizing tools like Miro or Figma for collaborative brainstorming and design processes enables teams to provide visual feedback in real time.

Benefits of Digital Collaboration:
1. **Increased Productivity**: Streamlined communication and organization lead to more efficient workflows.
2. **Flexibility**: Teams can work from anywhere, accommodating various schedules and time zones.
3. **Enhanced Innovation**: Diverse teams contribute different perspectives, fostering creativity and problem-solving.
4. **Real-Time Updates**: Instant access to information ensures everyone stays informed about project progress.
Challenges:
1. **Communication Barriers**: Misunderstandings can occur without non-verbal cues present in face-to-face

interactions.

2. **Over-Reliance on Technology**: Technical issues can disrupt workflows; having backup plans is essential.

3. **Distraction and Overload**: Too many tools can lead to confusion and reduced focus.

Best Practices for Effective Digital Collaboration:

1. **Set Clear Objectives**: Define goals and expectations for collaborative projects.

2. **Use the Right Tools**: Choose platforms that suit the team's needs and workflow.

3. **Regular Check-Ins**: Schedule consistent meetings to assess progress and address challenges.

4. **Encourage Engagement**: Foster a culture where all team members feel comfortable sharing ideas and feedback.

Future Trends:

1. **AI-Powered Collaboration**: Tools will increasingly use AI to analyze team dynamics and suggest improvements.

2. **Increased Focus on Cybersecurity**: As data sharing grows, so will the importance of protecting sensitive information.

3. **Virtual Reality Workspaces**: Immersive environments may enhance remote collaboration, simulating in-office interactions.

Digital collaboration ultimately reshapes how teams work together, breaking down geographical barriers and enabling more efficient workflows.

THIRTY-SEVEN
DIGITAL CITIZENSHIP

Digital citizenship refers to the responsible and ethical use of technology and the internet. It encompasses the skills, knowledge, and behaviors needed to navigate the digital world effectively and safely. Here's a detailed overview:

Key Components of Digital Citizenship:

1. Digital Literacy:

- Understanding how to use technology and digital tools effectively.
- Ability to search for, evaluate, and create information online.

2. Online Safety and Security:

- Protecting personal information and privacy online.
- Recognizing potential online threats like phishing, malware, and cyberbullying.

3. Ethical Use of Technology:

- Respecting copyright and intellectual property rights.
- Understanding the implications of spreading misinformation.

4. Digital Etiquette:

- Practicing respectful and responsible communication online.
- Being aware of how one's online behavior affects others.

5. Civic Engagement:

- Participating in online communities and discussions.
- Advocating for social issues through digital platforms.

6. Digital Responsibility:

- Taking accountability for one's actions in the digital space.
- Understanding the consequences of digital footprints.

Benefits of Digital Citizenship:
1. Empowerment: Individuals who practice good digital citizenship are better equipped to make informed decisions online.

2. Community Engagement: Encourages active participation in online communities, fostering collaboration and dialogue.

3. Safer Online Experiences: Understanding potential risks enhances personal security and promotes safer internet practices.

Challenges:

1. Digital Divide: Not everyone has equal access to digital technologies, creating disparities in digital citizenship education.

2. Rapid Technological Changes: Keeping up with new tools and platforms can challenge individuals to stay informed.

3. Misinformation: The spread of false information can undermine trust and challenge informed decision-making.

Best Practices for Promoting Digital Citizenship:

1. Education: Incorporating digital citizenship into school curricula to teach students about online behavior and safety.

2. Encourage Critical Thinking: Teaching individuals to critically evaluate sources and the information they encounter online.

3. Parental Guidance: Encouraging parents to discuss internet use with their children and model appropriate online behavior.

4. Community Programs: Organizing workshops and seminars to promote digital literacy in the community.

Future Trends:

1. Increased Focus on Privacy: As privacy concerns grow, digital citizenship will increasingly involve understanding data protection.

2. Technological Solutions: Emerging tools and platforms may provide resources for better educating users about digital rights and responsibilities.

3. Global Perspective: As digital citizenship becomes more recognized, approaches to teaching it may become more standardized worldwide.

Digital citizenship is essential in today's interconnected world, enabling individuals to interact responsibly, ethically, and safely online.

THIRTY-EIGHT

DIGITAL ETIQUETTE AND RESPONSIBILITIES

Digital etiquette and responsibilities are essential aspects of digital citizenship, guiding individuals on how to behave in online environments appropriately and ethically. Here's an in-depth look at both concepts:

Digital Etiquette

Digital etiquette, also known as netiquette, refers to the rules and guidelines for respectful and appropriate behavior online. Here are key components:

1. Respectful Communication:

- Use polite language and tone, avoiding aggressive or inflammatory comments.
- Be mindful of the impact of your words, as tone can be misinterpreted in written form.

2. Considerate Posting:

- Think before you post or share content, ensuring it is relevant and appropriate for the audience.
- Avoid posting harmful or inappropriate content, including personal attacks or hate speech.

3. Privacy Awareness:

- Respect others' privacy, avoiding sharing personal information without consent.
- Be cautious when discussing sensitive topics or sharing pictures/videos.

4. Acknowledgment and Attribution:

- Give credit to original creators when using or sharing their work, adhering to copyright laws.
- Properly reference sources of information, especially in academic or professional contexts.

5. Manners in Online Communication:

- Use proper grammar, spelling, and punctuation to convey professionalism.
- Use emojis and informal language judiciously, as they may not always be appropriate.

6. Listening and Respectful Discourse:

- Engage in discussions by listening to others' viewpoints, even if you disagree.
- Avoid dominating conversations, allowing space for others to share their opinions.

Digital Responsibilities

Digital responsibilities encompass the ethical and practical obligations of individuals when using technology. Here are key aspects:

1. Accountability:

- Own your actions online, recognizing that digital behavior can have real-world consequences.
- Address mistakes openly and learn from them rather than deflecting blame.

2. Safety and Security:

- Protect personal information by using strong passwords and enabling two-factor authentication.
- Be vigilant about online scams and phishing attempts, ensuring cybersecurity practices.

3. Critical Thinking:

- Analyze the information critically before sharing to prevent the spread of misinformation.
- Verify facts by consulting multiple reliable sources before forming opinions or making decisions.

4. Respecting Intellectual Property:

- Understand and adhere to copyright laws, using content legally and ethically.
- Avoid plagiarism by properly citing sources and using original ideas.

5. Promoting a Positive Online Environment:

- Participate constructively in discussions and contribute positively to online communities.
- Challenge negative behavior, such as bullying or harassment, when witnessed online.

6. Lifelong Learning:

- Stay informed about technology trends, online safety, and changes in digital etiquette.
- Embrace continuous learning to adapt to new tools and evolving online environments.

Practical Tips for Practicing Digital Etiquette & Responsibilities:

- **Pause Before You Post**: Take a moment to consider how your message may be received before sharing.
- **Set Privacy Settings**: Regularly review and adjust privacy settings on social media and online accounts.
- **Report Misconduct**: If you encounter harassment or inappropriate behavior, use reporting tools available on platforms.
- **Educate Others**: Share knowledge about digital etiquette and responsibilities with friends, family, or colleagues, fostering a positive online culture.
- **Lead by Example**: Model good digital behavior to encourage others to adopt similar practices.

Understanding and practicing digital etiquette and responsibilities are crucial for fostering a respectful and safe online community. By following these guidelines, individuals can contribute positively to the digital landscape, navigating it with integrity and respect.

THIRTY-NINE

PERSONAL AND ORGANIZATIONAL WEBSITES

Personal Websites

Definition: Personal websites are typically created by individuals to showcase their personal brand, skills, interests, and experiences. They can serve various purposes, such as portfolios, blogs, or resumes.

Key Features:

1. Portfolio Showcase: Display work samples, projects, and achievements relevant to career goals or personal interests.

2. Blog or Articles: Share thoughts, experiences, and expertise on specific topics, establishing authority and engaging visitors.

3. About Me Section: Provide a personal narrative, including background, education, and interests, helping visitors connect with the individual.

4. Contact Information: Offer ways for visitors to reach out, including email links, social media profiles, or contact forms.

5. Responsive Design: Ensure that the website is accessible and visually appealing across various devices, from desktops to smartphones.

Benefits:

- **Personal Branding**: Establish a unique online identity, enhancing professional visibility and opportunities.
- **Networking**: Connect with like-minded individuals, professionals, or potential employers through shared interests and experiences.
- **Skill Development**: Learn web design, content creation, and digital marketing by building and maintaining a personal website.

Organizational Websites

Definition: Organizational websites are created by businesses, non-profits, or institutions to communicate with stakeholders, provide information about services or products, and promote brand identity.

Key Features:

1. Homepage: Serve as the main entry point, showcasing the organization's mission, values, and primary offerings.

2. Service/Product Pages: Detail what the organization offers, including features, pricing, and benefits, with clear calls to action.

3. Blog or News Section: Share updates, industry insights, or thought leadership articles to engage and inform visitors.

4. Contact Page: Include multiple contact options, such as phone numbers, emails, social media links, and physical addresses.

5. User Testimonials/Reviews: Highlight positive feedback from customers or clients to build trust and credibility.

Benefits:

- **Visibility and Credibility**: Enhance the organization's online presence, making it easier for potential clients, partners, and customers to find information.
- **Communication Hub**: Provide a platform for disseminating information, updates, and news, fostering better communication with stakeholders.
- **Marketing Tool**: Utilize search engine optimization (SEO) strategies and digital marketing techniques to attract and retain customers.

Key Differences Between Personal and Organizational Websites

- **Purpose**: Personal websites focus on individual branding and self-presentation, while organizational websites emphasize the brand, services, and products of an organization.
- **Audience**: Personal websites target individuals, potential employers, and networking connections; organizational websites address customers, clients, partners, and the public.
- **Content**: Personal websites often feature creative work, personal experiences, and blogs, whereas organizational websites highlight services, industry information, and corporate communications.

In an increasingly digital landscape, both personal and organizational websites play pivotal roles in establishing online presence and engagement. Personal websites allow individuals to cultivate their brand and share their expertise, while organizational websites provide essential information and services to various stakeholders. Understanding the unique characteristics and benefits of each type of website is crucial for effectively leveraging them to achieve personal or organizational goals.